7/05

Sorrow & Solace

The Social World of the Cemetery

Philip Bachelor, Ph.D.

Death, Value and Meaning Series
Series Editor: John D. Morgan

Baywood Publishing Company, Inc.
AMITYVILLE, NEW YORK

Baywood Publishing Company, Inc.
26 Austin Avenue
Amityville, NY 11701
(800) 638-7819
E-mail: baywood@baywood.com
Web site: baywood.com

Library of Congress Catalog Number: 2004046303
ISBN: 0-89503-297-X (cloth)

Library of Congress Cataloging-in-Publication Data

Bachelor, Philip, 1955-
    Sorrow & solace : the social world of the cemetery / by Philip Bachelor.
        p. cm. -- (Death, value, and meaning series)
    Includes bibliographical references and index.
    ISBN 0-89503-297-X (cloth)
        1. Cemeteries. 2. Mourning customs. 3. Grief. 4. Bereavement. I. Title: Sorrow and solace. II. Title. III. Series.

GT3320.B23 2004
393--dc22

                                                                    2004046303

Contents

PART A

PART B

PART C

Acknowledgments

Several organizations and numerous individuals have contributed to and supported the compilation of this volume, which reflects little of my own ideas, but rather the shared knowledge and experiences of many.

Most of those to whom I am grateful shall remain anonymous. To the many mourners who allowed me to delve into their personal grief and explore their intimate experiences, beliefs and practices, I express my heartfelt appreciation and sincere thanks for the privilege of sharing such a momentous part of your lives.

I am particularly indebted to the Fawkner Crematorium & Memorial Park Trust members, and General Manager Mr. Ian Roddick, for extensive support of my various research and other professional endeavors. And I have appreciated encouragement and support from members of the Australasian Cemeteries & Crematoria Association, and of the Cemeteries and Crematoria Association of Victoria.

I am indebted to Dr. Neil Lipscombe and Dr. Jim Birckhead of Charles Sturt University for guiding me into the field of ethnographic social research. I am also grateful to Professor Allan Kellehear of La Trobe University for encouragement and guidance in developing my original manuscript, and to Emeritus Professor John Morgan and Mr. Stuart Cohen of Baywood Publishing Company for their interest and support in publication of this work.

Numerous staff, industry colleagues and friends have also assisted in various ways toward the completion of this work. But my greatest debt of gratitude is to my wonderful wife Jan, and to Emma, Lisa, and Sarah, who almost tolerate my obsessions, and with whom I share life's sorrow and solace.

Philip Bachelor

To every thing there is a season,
and a time for every purpose under the heaven:
A time to be born, and a time to die; . . .
A time to weep, and a time to laugh;
a time to mourn, and a time to dance; . . .

(Ecclesiastes 3:1-4)

"Sometimes I feel a little bit of sadness at the cemetery,
and other times I have a laugh and chuckle;
it depends on what I think about at the time.
If you think about a good time you sort of laugh and chuckle,
but if you're thinking about sad things then you will be sad."

(51-year-old, Australian, non-religious husband, bereaved 2 months)

Introduction

This book is about the importance of cemeteries in the lives of everyday mourners, and ways in which our bereaved give meaning to and draw value from their commemorative activities.

The death of someone dear to us is the most momentous life event that we are likely to ever experience. And in predominantly Christian societies, visiting the grave or memorial is a most common behavioral response to bereavement. Memorial sites provide vital connections to our deceased loved ones with whom we wish to maintain ongoing social bonds, and cemeteries are crucial places of deep healing and growth.

Literally millions of visits are made to cemeteries every day, but the extent of this activity and its personal values have long remained largely unrecognized. In opening up this issue, this volume represents an important contribution to contemporary knowledge of the phenomena of bereavement, mourning, and commemoration.

Large urban memorial parks are virtual hives of activity by recently bereaved persons, and they hold a place among the most visited places in Western communities. Some cemeteries, hosting literally millions of annual visits, are evidently more popular than many major tourist attractions.

Cemetery visitation is indeed a high-participatory, value-laden, expressive activity, and a most significant observable behavior of the recently bereaved.

CEMETERY VALUES

Sometimes there is far too much focus on merely the economic and historic values of cemeteries, while all too often the real rationale for cemeteries and their main community values remain unrecognized.

Society does not require us to build and operate a cemetery just because of some need for another business, or specifically to provide employment. Nor does any community establish a cemetery so that it will eventually have another historic museum.

It is well said that: "he who pays the piper calls the tune." Today, in many Western countries, including Australia, Canada, the United Kingdom and the United States, the only societal groups that pay for cemetery services are those of recently bereaved families. Logically then, they would appear to be the only legitimate groups with any right to call the tune. But the outside interests of vocal minorities are often given more consideration than the genuine needs of bereaved families having quite significant financial and emotional investments in a particular cemetery.

For over two decades I have listened to and observed tens of thousands of mourners rightfully expecting cemeteries to cater for their practical, emotional, and cultural needs. To these *bona fide* stakeholders—the only ones who actually pay for the existence of facilities and provision of services—the rationale of the cemetery is none other than to provide for their personal needs.

Their initial *practical* need is for the orderly disposition of the bodily remains of a family member. *Emotional* needs include an appropriately dignified funeral, an opportunity to commemorate the decedent so that recognition will remain through and possibly beyond the mortal life of the mourners, and the provision of an appropriate locus for revisiting memories and working through grief. *Cultural* needs include opportunities to observe traditional and contemporary family, community, religious or spiritual practices in the funeral, and in memorialization and ongoing visitation.

Meeting these needs must be the rationale of any cemetery authority hoping to provide a worthwhile service to its community. And so, to be effective, cemetery operators must become intimately familiar with, and truly understand, the personal needs of those of diverse backgrounds and bereaved through various circumstances.

BACKGROUND TO THE RESEARCH

On social introductions, and learning that I work in a cemetery, many have remarked that the job must be so easy because all of my clients are dead. My usual response is to inform them that they couldn't be more wrong. The deceased are not our clients; the families they leave behind are. And these survivors are not only very much alive and kicking, but often also screaming. I may go on to advise that our clients represent all nationalities and religions, come frequently in family groups at the time of greatest distress and emotional turmoil in their lives, and represent all relationships and losses through all conceivable circumstances. I might also add that we get only one chance at fully satisfying their primary service need, among those of many other families each day.

Rather than something so easily dismissed, cemetery management can be a highly challenging profession requiring the application of a range of business, social and environmental knowledge and skills with a sensitivity not usually required in many other service industries.

Episodic threats, armed security guards, and sneaking staff out through side entrances are not within most people's concept of running a cemetery. But not wishing to present an unduly distorted image, I hasten to add that the greatest proportion of management activity is directed toward supporting grieving families within a prevailing environment of relative peace.

The naivety of unfamiliar social acquaintances is to be expected. Far more surprising was my revelation just over a decade ago that the Australian and international cemeteries industries had little idea of who their clients actually were, let alone what clients' needs might be. No specific social data existed on the people now known to be paying around 32 million annual visits to Australia's 2,300 cemeteries. And the pervading industry attitude suggested that it would be insensitive and inappropriate to subject cemetery visitors to personal scrutiny.

I now recognize a combination of factors at play in the industry's reluctance to become acquainted with its clientele. Firstly, cemetery managers saw themselves as *facility operators*, rather than *service providers*. Many remained afraid of the mysteries of death, uncomfortable with the emotions of their clients, and unfamiliar with various religious and other cultural requirements.

Maintaining clients at a good arm's length meant that we did not have to become burdened by our clients' grief. Many managers felt they lacked the skills necessary to talk to grieving clients, and this was seen as the domain of professionally trained counselors. Others considered themselves too busy running the business to get involved in what they employed others to deal with. And some just wished to avoid emotional people who complain unreasonably and seek to dump their grief on someone else.

Other managers and directors considered that their own personal bereavement experiences provided adequate insight and empathy with the experiences of others. And some felt that from their experience they knew best the needs of mourners, who should even be grateful for such caring responsible management.

Far too many of authority considered cemeteries to be merely disposal places for cadavers or just historic museums, and much legislation still reflects this. There was little if any appreciation of the major community values of cemeteries. So empirical study of cemetery visitation and visitors' values and needs was greatly overdue.

For years now I have been discovering who visits whom, when, why, and how often. I have investigated who the cemetery industry's clients are, visiting behaviors and needs, how visitation is influenced by specific social factors (including age and sex of visitors, and relationships to the deceased), and by cultural factors (including perceived nationalities and religions of families).

In response to requests from other cemeteries, and with support of the Australasian Cemeteries & Crematoria Association, I found myself coordinating a series of studies at major cemeteries throughout Australia. And the total data were compiled to construct a national cemetery visitation profile. Collectively, the participating cemeteries provided almost 30% of all Australian burials and cremations, and the total survey sample comprised responses from 3,000 visitors.

This profile provided fascinating quantitative data on cemetery clients, from which many generalizations could be drawn. One's family religion and relationship to the decedent were found to be major determinants of visitation at all cemeteries, and the statistical significances of common social and cultural demographics were identified. However, these data revealed nothing of the personal experiences of individual mourners; this was yet to be acquired through further complementary qualitative research.

In-depth personal interviews with mourners of various religions and relationships to decedents were then conducted with informants purposively selected to approximate a cross-section of general cemetery visitors, as identified from the quantitative data. These interviews included discussion of issues such as impacts of bereavement, cemetery visitation activities, emotional experiences, and personal values of cemeteries, memorials, and visitation, across various social and cultural contexts.

Sorrow and solace were identified as the main groups of emotions experienced in association with cemetery visitation; and these emotions were found to be not necessarily exclusive of each other.

Sorrow & Solace: The Social World of the Cemetery presents major findings of these studies, offering fresh insights into practical bereavement and common personal values of the cemetery to those working their way through grief.

STRUCTURE OF THIS BOOK

Sorrow & Solace: The Social World of the Cemetery comprises three main parts. Part A lays a contextual foundation for the original research findings to be introduced later on. This first part reviews the evolution of the modern cemetery environment, looks at contemporary death, current concepts of bereavement and grief, and the research methods employed in the studies on which Parts B and C are based.

Part B presents major findings of a unique quantitative visitation study, and identifies the volume of visits, common visitation patterns, and the significance of common social and cultural attributes within cemetery visitation.

Part C then presents key findings of a qualitative bereavement study, and identifies personal values of the cemetery to mourners of diverse backgrounds. Major reasons for visitation and non-visitation, specific activities and emotions of visitors, and issues relating to common frequencies of visitation are all considered. Finally, key values of the cemetery to most mourners are identified.

I sincerely hope that this volume will help widely extend common understanding of contemporary bereavement and the needs of those who mourn. The work represents a significant reference for those seeking a broader understanding of longer-term practical bereavement; and it will be of particular value in guiding those in the caring professions and support services toward helping millions of mourners each year through the most difficult period of their lives.

Part A

The chapters presented in this first part identify key issues in the evolution of the modern cemetery environment, look at death today in a modern Western society, review experiences of bereavement, and consider current wisdom in the field of grief. Part A then concludes with an introduction to the research methodologies that were employed for the cemetery Visitation Study presented in Part B, and the Bereavement Study presented in Part C.

CHAPTER 1
Evolution of the Cemetery Milieu

This chapter introduces the modern, developed Western cemetery from an historical perspective, presenting a brief overview of major evolutionary influences on today's cemetery environment.

The milieu, or social environment, of cemeteries has evolved over many years in response to changing health, religious, political, technological, social, cultural, economic, and commercial concerns. Many changes have ushered in significant improvements for those acquiring cemetery services, such as graves and memorials, and also for non-paying visitors. But some changes have been imposed to meet external desires, without fully regarding the needs of the bereaved.

The practice of burying our dead appears to be as old as humanity itself. But the earliest known cremation to date was that of a young Australian Aboriginal woman, at Lake Mungo in New South Wales, approximately 26,000 years ago [1, 2]. Among the early Australians, funeral practices varied both spatially and temporally, with significant changes including vertical and prone entombment evident from burials spanning 7,000 years at one excavated cemetery [2].

The modern cemetery concept has emerged over the past 200 or so years, with distinct variations reflecting cultural diversity between various countries, provinces, and localities.

As Griffin and Tobin observe of the modern Australian scene:

> There are certainly similarities to practices in other countries, including the United Kingdom and the United States, but the differences are important [3, p. 2].

Today, practical variations, such as differing opinions on the "proper" orientation of graves, may even be found between different general cemeteries within the one town.

RECENT CENTURIES

Etlin observes that Western attitudes to death and the place of the cemetery have changed considerably over recent centuries [4]. And this has particularly been so since the late eighteenth century. Modern public cemeteries took their place alongside what had been almost exclusively the lot of churchyards and some private properties. Rapid population growth, industrialization, and urbanization then saw many cemeteries absorbed by early urban sprawl.

In some places, reuse of graves is reported to have been common practice. Trenches were sometimes dug for communal graves, and as cemeteries filled, new burials took place on top of earlier ones. Prior to common development of sewerage systems in urban environments, and separation of facilities such as abattoirs and domestic waste disposal, some cemeteries, as ready dumping grounds for these common urban wastes, were reported to be rather unpleasant and unsanitary places [4, 5].

Existing burial grounds and churches were overwhelmed when plague swept Britain in both 1348 and 1665 [6]. Emergency cemeteries had to be dug and many bodies were buried without coffins.

> Excavation of London's Royal Mint site in 1986 revealed the remains of victims of the 1348 plague buried up to five deep—in trenches no more than 2 meters deep [6, p. 14].

Etlin notes that, in Paris, a new concern for public hygiene emerged during the eighteenth century, presenting grave fear of the role of cemeteries and church burials in cultivating and spreading common diseases [4]. Major biochemical discoveries of the 1770s, including the discovery of oxygen and microbiology, heralded much of modern medical science with awareness of the principles of respiration and of parasitic disease. And growing community concerns further focused attention on the apparent problems of urban health.

Groundwater pollution from burial grounds and sewers was found to be a cause of London's first major cholera epidemic in 1831, and the English General Board of Health included graveyards in its official 1850 report as one of the causes of cholera [5, 7]. Evil miasmata hovering over burial grounds were reported to be responsible for everything from tarnishing silverware and spoiling food to causing fatal illnesses such as typhus, cholera, and diphtheria [4, 5]. And publicized medical opinions of the day evidently cultivated such concerns.

Around this time, traditional communal graves were apparently offending what Etlin describes as a newfound sense of public decency [4]. Out of these changing values and ideologies emerged the Elysium cemetery concept. Elysian fields, of ancient Greek mythology, were a paradise of rest for heroes favored by the gods. Later tradition envisaged the Elysium to comprise meadows circled by trees and crossed by streams, where all virtuous souls retired after death and roamed through evergreen bowers [8, 9].

These new cemeteries were to have important cultural as well as spiritual roles, according to Etlin, as virtuous citizens of all walks of life were to be honored by monuments and inscriptions, to inspire the living to at least equal the accomplishments of those before them [4]. They were to animate every citizen to a love of virtue and glory, and to excite in youthful minds an ardent desire of imitating those celebrated worthies [8]. And new cemeteries were to become schools of virtue, and to balance Christian and humanistic ideals [4]. These outdoor schools of history and philosophy would preach lessons to which none may refuse to listen, and which all that live must hear [9].

It became popular to establish new cemeteries on elevated sites, exposed to prevailing winds, enclosed within walls, and planted so as not to hinder air circulation [4]. They were also distanced from residential areas, though not so far as to make access difficult or expensive [5].

GARDEN CEMETERIES

In Paris, with continual reuse, the ground level in Cimetière des Innocents built up so much that in 1780 a wall eventually gave way spilling remains into adjacent property [4, 10]. In response, old Parisian cemeteries were subsequently cleared and the bones re-interred on display in subterranean catacombs. Today, these catacombs attract many thousands of tourists each year. A new wooded garden Cimetière du Père-Lachaise was established in 1804 and is generally credited with starting the rural cemetery movement subsequently popularized throughout the United States of America [4, 9, 11]. According to Etlin, Père-Lachaise, perhaps the most famous cemetery in the Western world, is a turning point in one thousand years of Western civilization [4].

Cemetery reformations similar to that in Paris then commenced in Britain at Low Hill General Cemetery, Liverpool, in 1825, and in the United States at Mount Auburn, Boston, in 1831 [4, 8-11].

The informal English estates, which served as models, included vast expanses of rolling grass with handsome trees that had replaced countless formal gardens during the eighteenth century. And instead of monuments and sculptures overshadowing horticulture, at Mount Auburn the emphasis was and is clearly on the supremacy of the landscape [9]. This rural cemetery concept, considered to be a radical departure from the crowded neglected seventeenth century crypts and graveyards within urban areas, quickly caught on [9]. The establishment of Mount Auburn was soon followed by the founding of other United States rural cemeteries, including Green-Wood, Brooklyn, in 1838 [10].

Within the United States, garden cemeteries were the forerunners of large-scale public open spaces near urban areas [10]. Churchyards initially served as public gathering places and were used as markets, forums, and malls. Keister reports that Andrew Downing, a promoter of public open space, visited Green-Wood in 1848 and remarked:

Judging from the crowds of people in carriages, and on foot, which I find
constantly thronging Green-Wood and Mount Auburn, I think it is plain
enough how much our citizens, of all classes, would enjoy public parks on a
similar scale. Indeed, the only drawback to these beautiful and highly kept
cemeteries, to my taste, is the gala-day air of recreation they present. People
seem to go there to enjoy themselves, and not to indulge in any serious
recollections or regrets. Can you doubt that if our large towns had suburban
pleasure grounds, like Green-Wood (excepting the monuments) ... they
would become the constant resort of the citizens, or that, being so, they would
tend to soften and allay some of the feverish unrest of business which seems to
have possession of most Americans, body and soul? [11, p. 28].

According to Keister, Downing kept hammering away at New York City officials
to develop a park patterned after the rural cemeteries, and finally had his way in
1853, when:

a 700 acre site (that eventually grew to 843 acres) was authorized to establish a
park in the center of New York City. Central Park was the first landscaped
park in America [11, p. 28].

RAILWAY ACCESS

Shifts away from cities brought corresponding changes in burial customs, and
in particular, transport of coffins and mourners to cemeteries. In the late nineteenth
century, railways were often considered appropriate means of access for both
funerals and subsequent visitation to cemeteries. Cemeteries could therefore be
sited away from cities. However, this involved a significant change from the
respectful tradition of slow conveyance of the deceased for burial [5].

Railway funerals were first introduced in England in 1854 with the
opening of a large, state-run cemetery in Woking, and the idea spread as far as
Australia, where the first such railway connection was made to Sydney's
Rookwood cemetery in 1867 [5].

COMPARTMENTALIZATION

Back in 1862, discriminatory compartmentalization of cemeteries by
religious denominations was being contested in Australia, and debate on this
issue continued for many years [12]. By the early 1890s, non-sectarian memorial
parks, such as Cypress Lawn at Colma, California, were being developed as a
more open, democratic alternative to church cemeteries and denominationally-
segmented public cemeteries [11]. However, many twentieth century cemeteries
were still laid out in religious divisions, and this generally remained the norm
until the 1980s.

CREMATION

A most significant change to take place in funeral practice was the legalization of cremation. But this did not come about quickly or easily. The cremation movement was initiated in Europe in the late nineteenth century. While specifically established cremationist organizations vigorously promoted this practice, it was generally considered "un-Christian" or "heathen" by many Anglo-Celtic Christians [13-15]. In 1886, an edict of the Roman Catholic Church officially condemned cremation, and it was not until 1963 that the Church's formal opposition to cremation was finally withdrawn [13, 14].

In 1895, an "illegal" cremation conducted on a beach in Victoria, Australia, received considerable press attention [5, 13, 16]. Nicol well illustrates the polarization of public opinion at the time with highly contrasting newspaper reports of the event. While the *Melbourne Age* described in embellished detail, "a most ghastly spectacle," the *Adelaide Observer* reported the same incident as a "decent and orderly" ceremony [5].

Common fears and suspicions, at least partly cultivated by church led antagonism, ensured that cremation once legalized did not gain rapid acceptance. But, though off to a slow start, acceptance did progressively grow throughout the twentieth century. Ultimately, modern crematoria housing purpose-built furnaces and with adjoining chapels for holding funeral services were built and commissioned in many modern cities prior to the Second World War.

Today, cremation continues to strengthen its position in Western societies, and particularly so where the grip of traditional practices including religion is lessening and environmental issues such as land-use are of growing concern (see Figure 1.1).

Over the years, cremation has increased in popularity to now account for almost 71% of all funerals in Great Britain, around 46% in Canada, and around 27% in the United States, as shown in Figure 1.1. It currently represents around 55% of services in Australia. By comparison, the proportion of cremations in Japan is currently over 99%, but comprise just a fraction of services in strongly Catholic countries, such as Ireland at less than 6%, and Italy at less than 7% [17]. To date, the Orthodox Church has managed to keep Greece crematoria-free, but this position now looks shaky in the face of increasing pressures of modernization.

MEMORIAL PARKS

European and American garden cemeteries ultimately provided inspiration for, and influenced design and development of memorial parks in other countries.

In Los Angeles, Forest Lawn Memorial Park was established as the first full lawn cemetery [11, 18, 19]. Mitford credits Forest Lawn's creator, Hubert Eaton, as probably having more influence on trends in the modern cemetery industry than any other human being [20]. According to Llewellyn, when Hubert

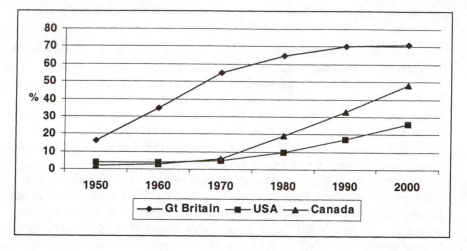

Figure 1.1 Proportions of cremations in selected countries over recent decades. **Sources:** Cremation Society of Great Britain 2000 [23] and Cremation Association of North America 2003 [24].

Eaton conceived his "memorial-park plan" in 1917, he transformed the way cemeteries were operated and viewed by society [19]. Mitford considers that not only was the Memorial Park idea born with Dr. Eaton's creed, but that the lengthened shadow of his genius subsequently crept over much of the cemetery land in the United States, to span oceans, extending to Hawaii and even to Australia [20].

MAUSOLEA

The term "mausoleum," for a structure usually housing above-ground crypts, originated with the tomb of King Mausoleus of Caria, in Asia Minor, a site now known as Halicarnassus in southwest Turkey. The magnificent sculptured tomb of Mausoleus, erected around 350 B.C. and destroyed in 1402, was considered one of the seven wonders of the ancient world [21].

Although having been around for many hundreds of years, entombment in slightly more modest mausoleum crypts became quite popular in Western countries during the twentieth century, and particularly in places of Italian immigration. As well as the earlier provision of individual family mausolea, elaborate community buildings have been available in the United States since at least the 1920s. Then with mausoleum crypts being associated with many popular personalities, this method has ultimately been adopted by people of diverse cultural backgrounds in North America, and is now gaining broader popularity in other countries.

Today, public mausolea usually provide hundreds, or even thousands, of crypts within one building. These grand, multilevel structures are further changing the current face of Western cemeteries and ushering in even more recent variation in contemporary cemetery entombment and memorialization.

CONCLUSION

Linden-Ward considers that over the last century and a half, Americans have created for themselves cemeteries that reflect their own notions of death, nature, individualism, family, community, and commemoration, worthy of a distinctive national historic consciousness [8]. A review of the world scene suggests that everywhere people are similarly creative in this respect, and have developed cemeteries that similarly reflect their respective cultures.

Etlin effectively sums up the processes at work in the evolving cemetery milieu [4].

> Despite all of the transformations in form and use, the cemetery always furnished a landscape, either architectural or horticultural, as well as metaphysical, which reflected the underlying bonds and tensions of social and individual life [4, p. 368].

And so, today, the cemetery continues in its role, responding to ever changing societal and personal needs.

On this point we conclude our summary of the evolution of the modern cemetery social environment. The next chapter looks at contemporary death, including when, why, and where deaths most commonly occur today.

REFERENCES

1. J. Flood, *Archaeology of the dreamtime,* Collins, Sydney, 1983.
2. J. P. White and J. F. O'Connell, *A prehistory of Australia, New Guinea and Sahul,* Academic Press, Sydney, 1982.
3. G. M. Griffin and D. Tobin, *In the midst of life . . .: The Australian response to death* (2nd ed.), Melbourne University Press, Melbourne, 1997.
4. R. A. Etlin, *The architecture of death,* MIT Press, Massachusetts, 1984.
5. R. Nicol, *At the end of the road: Government, society and the disposal of human remains in the nineteenth and twentieth centuries,* Allen & Unwin, Australia, 1994.
6. L. Spinney, The way of all flesh, *New Scientist, 146*(1971), pp. 12-15, 1995.
7. C. Spicer, Boroondara: Australia's first landscaped garden cemetery, *Heritage Australia,* pp. 3-7, Winter 1991.
8. B. Linden-Ward, The heritage of Mount Auburn, reprinted by Mount Auburn Cemetery courtesy of *Cemetery Management Magazine,* January 1986.
9. J. Howard, The garden of earthly remains, reprinted by Mount Auburn Cemetery courtesy of *Horticulture, The Magazine of American Gardening,* September 1987.
10. D. Keister, Preserving nature's handiwork: Cemeteries serve the living and the dead, *American Cemetery,* pp. 26-32, January 1999.

11. D. Keister, A brief history of the community mausoleum, *American Cemetery, 69*(9), pp. 20-52, 1997.

12. R. Nicol, *Fairway to heaven: The story of Enfield, Australia's first lawn cemetery*, Enfield General Cemetery Trust, Adelaide, 1997.

13. S. Zelinka, *Tender sympathies: A social history of Botany Cemetery*, Hale & Iremonger, Sydney, 1991.

14. C. Sagazio, *Cemeteries: Our heritage*, National Trust of Australia (Victoria), Melbourne, 1992.

15. A. W. Ata, *Bereavement & health in Australia: Gender, psychological, religious and cross-cultural issues*, David Lovell, Melbourne, 1994.

16. D. Chambers, *100 years of Le Pine*, Hyland House, Melbourne, 1994.

17. International Cremation Federation, International cremation statistics, *Pharos International, 68*(4), pp. 26-37, 2002.

18. Forest Lawn Memorial-Parks, *A place for the living*, Forest Lawn Memorial-Park Association, Glendale, California, 1994.

19. J. F. Llewellyn, *A cemetery should be forever: The challenge to managers and directors*, Tropico, Glendale, California, 1998.

20. J. Mitford, *The American way of death*, Penguin, Middlesex, 1965.

21. K. W. Joyce and I. I. Roddick, *Mausoleums*, Report to the Trustees of Fawkner Crematorium & Memorial Park, 1995.

22. J. A. Walter, *The revival of death*, Routledge, London, 1994.

23. Cremation Society of Great Britain, Progress of cremation in England & Wales and Scotland, *Directory of crematoria*, 2000.

24. Cremation Association of North America, (2003). Available online at: cremationassociation.org/docs/WebHistData

CHAPTER 2
Death Today

This chapter presents a brief glimpse at aspects of death today, including when, why, and where deaths most commonly occur within a modern Western society. Contemporary death, which is the primary reason for the provision of cemeteries, is reviewed by age, gender, cause, and place.

Based on the current mean age at death of 79 years, and each decedent having 25 close relatives (including surviving siblings, children, grandchildren, nieces, and nephews), it is estimated that within Australia, and by inference other countries with similar life expectancies and family structures, around one in six of the population suffers the loss of a family member each year. Many more will experience the death of a less close relative, friend, or associate.

WHEN WE DIE

More males than females die at all ages under 80 years of age, as shown in Figure 2.1. In Australia, the current average life expectancy at birth is around 76 years for males and 82 years for females. In the United States, it is around 74 years for males and 80 years for females, while in the United Kingdom, it is around 75 years for males and 80 years for females. Japan currently offers one of the greatest life expectancies, with the average Japanese male attaining around 77 years and the average female reaching around 83 years of age [1, 2].

During the 20-39-year-old period, within Australia, the male to female death ratio is almost three to one. Factors involved include the higher risk activities of young males, including motor accidents (accounting for around two-and-a-half male deaths to every one female death), and the significantly higher incidence of male suicide (accounting for almost four male deaths to every one female death).

While attempts at self-harm are no more common among males than females, males are more inclined to employ less-forgiving methods, such as the use of firearms and hanging. Female attempts are more likely to involve less reliable means, such as the use of sedatives and wrist cutting. However, at least within

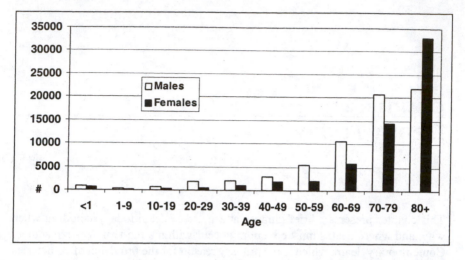

Figure 2.1 Deaths in Australia during 1999 by age and sex.
Source: Australian Bureau of Statistics 3302.0 [1].

Australia over the past few years, carbon-monoxide poisoning (from motor exhausts) has become a most popular suicide method for both sexes.

WHY WE DIE

The male death rate is higher than that of females for most leading causes of death (Figure 2.2). However, for some causes the number of female deaths typically exceeds the number of male deaths. These are cerebrovascular disease (stroke) and organic mental disorders (including senile dementia), both of which are usually associated with older age groups in which females predominate [3, 4].

Accidents are the leading cause of death for those under 45 years of age. Malignant neoplasms (cancers) are the second leading cause among this group except for those aged 15-24, where it is suicide. For those aged 45 years and over, neoplasms and heart disease are the leading causes [3]. The category "All other causes" includes diseases of other organs, infectious and parasitic diseases, perinatal deaths, poisonings, violence, and ill-defined conditions [3, 4].

WHERE WE DIE

Numerous authors on death and bereavement remark on the "institutionalization" of death through an evident historical shift from the most common place of death being the traditional home bed, to death more typically occurring in a hospital or similar institution. Some writers have postulated figures ranging from "over half" to "90%" of contemporary deaths occurring in hospitals and other

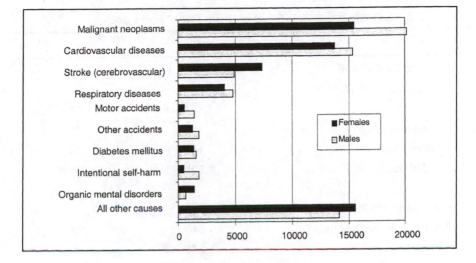

Figure 2.2 Deaths in Australia during 2000 by cause and sex.
Source: Australian Bureau of Statistics 3303.0 [3].

institutions [5-8]. But none of these reports refer to any specific data from which their respective figures may have been drawn.

An attempt has now been made to shed some light on this trend, drawing on available cremation data. However, it is recognized that precisely where we die may vary to some degree between countries, states, and sociocultural groups.

Cremation application forms for the years 1990 and 2000 were reviewed, at a major Australian memorial park providing slightly more cremations than burials, because these forms record the place of death. In urban Australia, with strong social welfare and public health systems, choice between burial and cremation is rarely based on economics, and paupers may be either buried or cremated by States, depending on the preference of any relatives or friends. The data drawn from this source is summarized in Table 2.1 and graphically illustrated in Figure 2.3.

The sample indicates that around 56% of those cremated in 2000 died in hospitals. And, when added to the sample deaths having occurred in hospices and nursing homes, it becomes evident that at least 78% of the total sample deaths occurred in some institution.

The recognized trend away from traditional home deaths is apparent from the decline of 22% to 18% over the past decade. And this directly correlates to an increase in hospital deaths from 51% to 56%, and all known institutionalized deaths from 72% to 78%, for the same period.

Table 2.1 Shift in Place of Death Over Recent Decade

	N	%
Place of Death 1990		
Hospice/nursing home	605	21
Hospital	1,444	51
Own residence	607	22
Other place	165	6
Totals	**2,821**	**100**
Place of Death 2000		
Hospice/nursing home	544	22
Hospital	1,376	56
Own residence	458	18
Other place	99	4
Totals	**2,477**	**100**

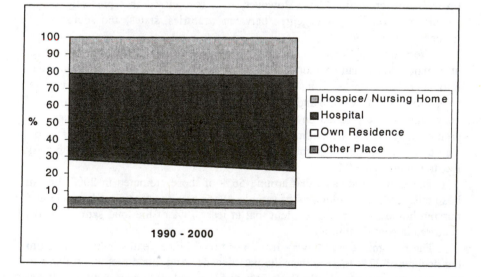

Figure 2.3 Shift in place of death over recent decade.

The available data relating to cremation suggests that around 80% of deaths currently occur in hospitals and other institutions; and this trend appears to be increasing.

Now that we have a better idea of who dies, when, why, and where, the next chapter will present an overview of current concepts of bereavement and grief.

REFERENCES

1. Australian Bureau of Statistics, *Deaths Australia 1999,* Cat. No. 3302.0, ABS, Canberra, 2000.
2. Australian Bureau of Statistics, *2001 Year book Australia,* Cat. No. 1301.0, A.G.P.S., Canberra, 2001.
3. Australian Bureau of Statistics, *Causes of death Australia 1998,* Cat. No. 3303.0, ABS, Canberra, 1999.
4. Australian Bureau of Statistics, *2003 Year book Australia,* Cat. No. 1301.0, A.G.P.S., Canberra, 2003.
5. J. A. Walter, *The revival of death,* Routledge, London, 1994.
6. A. W. Ata, *Bereavement & health in Australia: Gender, psychological, religious and cross-cultural issues,* David Lovell, Melbourne, 1994.
7. A. Deveson, Everyone a customer, in *The Penguin book of death,* G. Carey and R. Sorenson (eds.), Penguin, Melbourne, 1997.
8. G. M. Griffin and D. Tobin, *In the midst of life . . .: The Australian response to death* (2nd ed.), Melbourne University Press, Melbourne, 1997.

CHAPTER 3

Concepts of Bereavement and Grief

Toward appreciating the ongoing values of cemeteries to mourners, it is imperative to acquire an empathetic, though objective, understanding of the experiences of bereavement and grief. This chapter therefore presents an overview of popular and contemporary bereavement theories, conceptual ideas of the process of grief and its accommodation in the life of mourners, and a brief look at the relationship between grief and trauma.

BEREAVEMENT THEORIES

To help understand what happens to us when a person significant to us dies, several explanatory models of bereavement are postulated by numerous bereavement researchers and theorists. Popular approaches include psychodynamic, attachment, crisis, and disease theories.

Psychodynamic theory is based on work of pioneering psychoanalyst Sigmund Freud (1856-1939) [1]. This approach recognizes a need to relinquish a tie, but that letting go involves considerable pain [2]. Bringing forth and reviewing memories allows the mourner to withdraw ties to complete their grieving, so that emotional energy can then be regained and invested in other relationships [2-5].

Attachment theory draws on Freudian theory and interpersonal dynamics, pertaining to the individual's role transition within a social group. Theorists consider separation anxiety with the severing of strong attachment bonds [2-5]. Bowlby sees falling in love as the emotion of forming a social bond, loving as the emotion of maintaining such, and grief as the emotion of losing the bond [6].

Crisis theory suggests that the death of a significant other disturbs the survivor's homeostasis, and is therefore a stressful event. And in their crisis, the bereft is in danger of becoming disorganized and suffering physiological impacts [2, 3]. Alternatively, it is suggested that the bereft may then concentrate energies on reorganization and coping to the extent that pre-existing, latent problems may be resolved, thus providing positive change [2]. A crisis may be considered a major life stress of limited duration, which endangers mental health [7].

Disease theory considers grief to be a pathogenic syndrome, involving somatic distress. The process of wounding and subsequent healing experienced by the bereaved is seen as being similar to that experienced with physical injury. This medical model proposes that it is useful to think of abnormal behavior as disease [8]. Bereavement is also seen to bring on, or complicate, existing physical or psychological conditions [3, 7]. Though disease theory and its use of medical analogies is rejected by some, such as Attig [9], Parkes argues that grief *is* a common mental illness and that non-acceptance of this stems from incorrect and limited, but popular, ideas of what constitutes mental illness [7].

From any review of multiple theories of bereavement and grief, we must conclude that there is certainly more than one way to view the phenomena. And while each approach does have its critics, and may be incomplete, each does represent an important contribution to our broader understanding of grief.

Theories may pass into and out of fashion, but should not be totally discarded unless they have been fully debunked and found useless or even detrimental. I suggest that such is not yet the case with any of the above theoretical ideas. In this chapter then, we shall maintain an open position on all and value their contribution.

Each model permits researchers, clinicians, and mourners to understand various aspects of grief and to communicate more effectively through widely shared meanings. Grief is perhaps too complex to be adequately understood from any singular current theoretical perspective, and so the search for greater understanding and the construction of perhaps more complex models are evidently still necessary.

GRIEF PROCESSES

The phenomena of bereavement and grief are recognized as common across human cultures [3, 7, 10]. In all known societies, grief is expressed following a death, women cry and keen, anger and aggression are common, and fears of the dead body and spirit exist [3, 7].

Lindemann is generally credited with first proposing recognizable stages of grief [5, 9, 11]. He differentiated normal grief reactions from what he considered to be abnormal or morbid grief [11]. Attig notes that Lindemann originally identified three stages of grief, Bowlby proposed three alternative phases, Engel put forward his six stage idea, Kübler-Ross proposed a different five-stage process for the dying person, and Parkes modified Bowlby's phases to become four [9]. Numerous variations on these proposals have been postulated by other writers.

It is now commonly agreed that grief may involve a process of three or more recognizable phases. However, various contemporary opinions remain on the number and definitions of such phases. For example, Westberg presents a complete set of all 10 stages in his "constructive approach to the problem of loss" [12].

The following comparative outline of various proposed phases of grief reveals shifts in leading opinions and commonalities among various notions:

Lindemann, 1944 [11]:
1. Shock and disbelief
2. Acute mourning
3. Resolution

Bowlby, 1961 [13]:
1. Urge to recover the lost object
2. Disorganization and despair
3. Reorganization

Engel, 1964 [14]:
1. Shock and disbelief
2. Development of awareness
3. Restitution
4. Resolution of the loss
5. Idealization
6. Outcome

Kübler-Ross, 1969 [15]:
1. Denial and isolation
2. Anger
3. Bargaining
4. Depression
5. Acceptance

Parkes, 1974 [16]:
1. Numbness
2. Yearning and searching
3. Disorganization and despair
4. Reorganization

Sanders, 1989 [17]:
1. Shock—the impact of grief
2. Awareness of loss
3. Conservation—withdrawal
4. Healing—the turning point
5. Renewal

Shuchter and Zisook, 1993 [18]:
1. Initial shock, disbelief and denial
2. Acute mourning, somatic and emotional discomfort, and social withdrawal
3. Culminating period of restitution

Rando, 1993 [5]:

Avoidance Phase
1. Recognize the loss

Confrontation Phase
2. React to the separation
3. Recollect and re-experience the deceased and the relationship
4. Relinquish old attachments to the deceased and the old assumptive world

Accommodation Phase
5. Readjust to move adaptively into the new world without forgetting the old
6. Reinvest

Parkes, 1996 [7]:
1. The trauma response
2. The grief response
3. The psychosocial transition

It is evident from this range of ideas that the more recent process proposed by one of the most respected current authorities on bereavement (i.e., Parkes [7]) is virtually identical to that first proposed over 50 years earlier by Lindemann.

What emerges as a common pattern among the generally accepted processes of grief is well described by Attig.

> We are told that when we grieve, we are first hit hard by our bereavement. We are then immersed in the full impact of intense and often nearly over-whelmingly painful experiences. Eventually, however, we achieve some kind of new equilibrium in living as if we had been washed up on shore as if having nearly drowned [9, p. 42].

Common agreement of initial impact and eventual accommodation of loss is to be found within virtually all concepts of typical grief. However, between the genesis and diminution of intense grief remains a highly variable transition process.

Several authors caution their readers, particularly therapists, against taking grief staging too literally and attempting to fix a subject at a particular place on any proposed continuum [2, 3, 5, 7, 12, 17, 18]. As Attig maintains, we do not fall into lockstep as we grieve, or lose our individuality [9].

Shuchter and Zisook agree that grief is not a linear process with concrete boundaries, but rather a composite of overlapping fluid phases that vary from person to person [18]. It is commonly held today that phases of grief should only be regarded as general, flexible guidelines. Individuals may pass forwards and backwards between the phases, or become partially or completely locked in one or another [3]. There are considerable differences from one person to another as regards both the duration and the form of each phase [7]. So it is well suggested that dying and grieving are too complex and contradictory to be encapsulated in neat stages [19].

Each person grieves differently in different circumstances. Westberg considers no one has ever grieved exactly the same because no two people face even the same kind of loss in the same way [12]. A young mother, in my own naturalistic Bereavement Study [20], spoke of the difference between her own grieving and that of her husband.

> It's difficult, in the sense that everyone grieves differently. Just because I was her Mum and he was her Dad, doesn't mean that we're grieving in the same way. I found that I went through real anger. I hated everything and everyone—and God. How could this happen to me? At the same time, he was still just crying and sad. He couldn't understand why I was so angry. So you go through these different phases differently.
>
> *27-year-old, Australian Catholic mother,*
> *bereaved 10 months*

Many factors may combine to determine the outcomes of grief. Worden identifies determinants of grief as who the person was, the nature of the attachment, mode of death, historical antecedents, personality variables, and social variables [21]. These determinants of the outcome of bereavement may also be categorized into antecedent, concurrent, and subsequent factors. According to Parkes, antecedent determinants include our relationship with the deceased, childhood and later experiences, prior life crises and mode of death. Concurrent determinants include gender, age, personality, socio-economic status, nationality and religion. And subsequent determinants include social support or isolation, secondary stresses and emergent opportunities [7].

To Raphael, factors affecting the outcome of bereavement include:

> the pre-existing relationship between the bereaved and the deceased, the type of death, the response of the family and social network, concurrent stress or crises, previous losses, and sociodemographic factors such as age, sex, religion, culture, occupation and economic position [3, p. 62].

Our emotional attachment to the decedent is perhaps the most crucial factor in grieving. As Weiss observes, grief results from the loss of *primary* relationships, which he also calls relationships of attachment, but not from others, which he further categorizes as relationships of community [22]. For example, we may have a strong relationship of attachment with a close family member, and a less close relationship of community with a friend or associate. Weiss considers that differences in the severity and persistence of grief are usually experienced between the two relationships [22].

SOCIOLOGICAL PERSPECTIVES

If bereavement is considered to be the disruption by death of a significant relationship, then it is primarily a *sociological* phenomenon. It may produce apparent physiological and psychological manifestations, but it has a complex sociological nature, which has received too little focus and therefore remains less understood. Psychology has so far contributed more than any other discipline to our current knowledge of this most perplexing of human conditions, and common somatic responses to the death of another are also quite well understood. But, as yet, adequate sociological understanding of what is evidently a major sociological issue still remains forthcoming, though the work has begun.

A refreshing perspective that challenges much accepted wisdom is presented by Walter [19]. Focusing on the British hospice movement and bereavement counseling, Walter relates current death, funeral, and bereavement practices to social theories of modernity and post-modernity.

Walter considers we have experienced a "dying of death" through rationalization, medicalization, secularization, and individualism, and in response are now seeing a massive revival of death with two strands. He suggests that experts now control grief, and the late-modern strand replaces control through medical understanding with control through psychological understanding. But he believes the late-modern package is now being rejected because of its arrogance and because research is showing that people do not die or grieve in neat stages. He suggests that the post-modern strand places private feelings firmly onto the public agenda—in medical training, hospital routines, and the media—thus challenging the authority of experts. Collectively, Walter labels the two strands "neo-modern" [19].

He is critical of stage theories of grief, considering that dying and grieving are too complex and contradictory to be encapsulated in neat stages, and suggests that the function of stage theories is mainly to reassure students who have yet to encounter these experiences. He strongly rejects Kübler-Ross' stages, citing Klass [23] in suggesting that:

> In conflating hard data, personal involvement and a message that will save the world, Kübler-Ross has written not so much a scientific monograph offering testable hypotheses as a persuasive religious/political tract [19, p. 71].

It is very difficult for practitioners not to be influenced by psychosocial theories that provide reassuring generalizations about how people die and grieve, according to Walter. He challenges the assumptions of "several leading social scientists" that death is inherently terrifying, and we therefore need the comfort of religion and tradition. The popular focus on letting go in each case is also challenged, suggesting that counselors and psychologists who go on about the need to let go may for some mourners simply be compounding delayed grief.

> It may be that for many bereaved people in the West (not just those who have lost a child) their need is not to let go, for they know perfectly well that the deceased is dead. Their need is to be assured that they can keep the deceased in some compartment of their mind and heart. For them, a model in which grief results in keeping the deceased in some form . . . may be more helpful than standard Western models in which grief is resolved by an eventual letting go of the deceased and therapy is geared towards that end [19, p. 83].

According to Walter, at least in some cases, counseling and self-help groups may even collude with the private modern way of death, keeping grief conveniently out of the everyday way so that life can go on as though death did not exist. He suggests that a mass education campaign to teach everyone how to listen and support bereaved individuals would be more constructive than training skilled counselors. But he is realistic about the comparative ease of constructing self-help groups and pairs of lonely individuals as opposed to any attempt at reconstructing community [19].

Walter concludes that differences in grieving may be attributed to different social models, suggesting that Americans tend to construct themselves in a more modern/post-modern way, while Europeans do so in a more traditional way. He points out that it is not uncommon when a child dies for the (neo-modern) parents to grieve differently from the (modern) grandparents. If the parents have an expressive style, and the grandparents a stoical style, then their mutual incomprehension can add to the burden of grief of each other [19].

From the United States, Attig presents a further fresh perspective [9]. He considers grieving to be an active process by which we work our way through crises in self-identity and disruptions in our usual behavior patterns, to develop alternatives. According to Attig, in seeking comfort and understanding, many mourners turn to books on grieving but are ultimately disappointed. In response, he offers his idea of grieving as a process of "relearning the world." For this purpose he divides the world into our physical surroundings, our social world (relationships with other survivors), our personal selves, and our relationship with the deceased [9].

Attig suggests that grieving is not a process of passively living through stages, nor a clinical problem to be managed or solved by others. He believes that loss challenges us to relearn. Grieving is an active, coping process of relearning how to be and act in a world where loss transforms the fabric of our lives. Our assumptive world may be crushed, and a new world (or a new self) requires construction. According to Attig, ideas of stages or phases of grief, and medical analogies, both wrongly suggest that we come to an end in our grieving as we either complete the stages or at last recover. He strongly rejects ideas of grieving as passive, and suggests it is vital that we embrace notions of it as active. He recognizes bereavement as a helpless, wrenching deprivation and refers to this imposition as "choice-less," but he insists that grieving is not.

> Grieving, as coping, requires that we respond actively, invest energy, and address tasks. Among other things, coping requires that we come to terms with our grief emotion [9, p. 33].

Attig also questions the appropriateness of disease theory and its use of medical analogies. He suggests that terms such as "symptoms" of grief, "healing," and "recovery" erroneously suggest there is something wrong or abnormal about us when we grieve. He considers this doesn't ring true with many of us as we experience grieving as the quite normal thing to do when someone dies. Attig's concept of relearning the world includes relearning our physical surroundings, our social world (including relationships with survivors), ourselves, and our relationship with the deceased [9].

ACCOMMODATION OF GRIEF

It is well said of bereavement that you don't get over it, you just get used to it [22]. However, the hallmark of the restitution stage, according to Shuchter and Zisook, is the ability of the bereaved to recognize that they have grieved and can now return to work, re-experience pleasure, and seek the companionship and love of others [18].

The concept of "grief-work," introduced by Freud, involves the mourner working their way through a series of essential tasks [1, 21]. Parkes considers that in this respect, grieving is a creative activity—a gradual piecing together of the pieces of a jigsaw that, eventually, will enable us to find an image and a place in our lives for the people we have loved and lost [7]. Through this active process, says Attig, we work our way through crises in self-identity and disruptions in our usual behavior patterns and develop alternatives [9]. He even suggests that some mourners may need to be motivated to resist the attractions of remaining in grief, and to begin to address the tasks of grieving.

It has been proposed that grieving follows a predictable pattern, and that healing is attained if one allows him/her self to experience each step [3, 24]. Although it is generally acknowledged that the time taken to complete grief varies with the individual and degree of intimacy with the deceased, some authors (for example Raphael and O'Connor) do still offer typical time frames as a guide for major stages [3, 24].

Some theorists caution their readers against the ready use of terms such as "recovery," but do recognize such in terms of a return of ordinary functioning [2, 22]. Reasonable expectations of ordinary functioning, postulated by Weiss include:

Ability to give energy to everyday life,

Psychological comfort, as demonstrated by freedom from pain and distress,

Ability to experience gratification—to feel pleasure when desirable, hoped for, or enriching events occur,

Hopefulness regarding the future; being able to plan and care about plans, and,

Ability to function with reasonable adequacy in social roles, such as spouse, parent and member of the community [22, pp. 277-278].

Accommodation of bereavement within one's life involves processes identified by Weiss as cognitive acceptance, emotional acceptance, and identity change.

Cognitive acceptance occurs, as the mourner appears to develop a satis-factory account of the causes of the loss event. The absence of a satisfactory account seems to leave the bereaved anxiously perplexed, searching for contributions to the death, perhaps made by themselves or others. *Emotional acceptance* seems to require a neutralization of specific memories and asso-ciations which might otherwise paralyze normal functioning. As each emotion-laden memory and association is confronted, a reduction of associated pain occurs until tolerance for the memory is developed. And *identity change* occurs as the mourner develops a new image of his/herself and sees their connection to the deceased as part of his/her past. New commitments to new relationships help facilitate a perceived change of identity [22].

Numerous theorists recognize a distinction between what are generally termed "normal" and "abnormal" grief responses [2, 3, 5, 7, 25, 26]. But as Weiss suggests, in the absence of any universally accepted criteria for ordinary levels of effective functioning, researchers find it very difficult to define just what is normal and abnormal in grief and recovery [22]. We are reminded by Walter that norms (in the prescriptive sense) are derived not from religion or tradition, but from what is normal (in the statistical sense) [19]. He goes on to suggest that it is therefore the physician, the psychologist, and the statistician who can tell us how we ought to die and ought to grieve.

In reality, we all make judgments about what we consider to be "normal" and whether certain behavior fits within our own and shared concepts. But these are always imperfect arbitrary concepts; they are ultimately our personal value judgments.

According to Parkes, atypical grief may include chronic grief, delayed grief, anxiety and panic attacks, self-blame, hypochondria, and hysteria [7]. He suggests that anger and guilt are particularly likely to follow the dissolution of an ambiv-alent relationship and, because of their destructive nature, to lead to pathological forms of grief.

When the processes of resolving a loss do not occur, or where grief is distorted and a delayed pattern predominates, then it may be seen as patho-logical [4, 5]. Pathological outcomes of bereavement are identified by Raphael to include general symptomatology, psychosomatic disorder, depression, other psychiatric or psychosocial disorder, altered relationship patterns, vulnerability to loss, and mortality [3].

Rando considers that as grief is a natural expectable reaction, then its absence, when warranted by factors circumscribing a loss, is therefore abnormal and indicative of pathology [5]. The U.S. Institute of Medicine notes this contention, but is unsure of its validity [2]. Rando further suggests that in the event of some compromise, distortion or failure of the process of mourning, the potential outcomes include mental disorders, physical disorders, and even death [5].

Several morbid, or pathological, patterns of grief are identified in the literature. Prolonged severe grief, or chronic grief, is considered by some to be the most common type [2, 22]. Other pathological forms include absent, delayed, inhibited, distorted, conflicted, and unanticipated grief [3, 5]. Grief may be considered absent when the intensity of effects is too great, or the coping ability too weak, so that a rejecting defense mechanism may result; and delayed grief implies the emergence of grief-like symptoms, months or even years after apparently absent grief [2, 4].

Several researchers report on some people getting stuck in one stage or another and never moving on to the final stage of acceptance and rebuilding their lives [2, 3, 24]. Those most likely to become stuck in pathological grief reactions are thought to be those whose pre-bereavement response patterns were to avoid confrontation and to seek escape from difficult situations [2].

Osterweis, Solomon, and Green also found that pathological grief occurs where major positive reinforcement is lost from one's life, as is often the case in the death of a spouse. It is suggested that, with the loss of the strongest relationship of attachment and dependence, life can appear meaningless and all actions may be concluded as futile. Consequently, positive actions which would help alleviate stress may be avoided, thus compounding the situation [2].

Among 171 people referred to Parkes in recent years for the treatment of psychiatric problems following bereavement, he reports that 45% had lost a spouse (35% a husband, 10% a wife), 22% had lost a parent, 14% a child, and 11% had lost people of other relationships. The remaining 9% had experienced multiple bereavements [7].

Parkes also compared widows who sought to repress or avoid grief, by showing little or no emotional response during the first week of bereavement, with other initial responses. Those who engaged in little formal mourning, and avoided visiting the grave or crematorium, ultimately suffered more psychological and physical problems than those who "broke down" in the first week. Physical symptoms of those who held back included headaches, palpitations, insomnia, and alopecia, and these widows also became more psychologically disturbed around the anniversary of death [7].

The most characteristic feature of grief is not prolonged depression, but acute and episodic pangs of severe anxiety and psychological pain, according to Parkes [7]. Brief episodes of acute grief may be triggered by anything that resurrects personal memories or emphasizes the absence of the decedent. And, according to Rando, these Subsequent Temporary Upsurges of Grief (or STUG reactions) may normally occur long after a death and are not necessarily indicative of abnormal grief [5].

As we endeavor to come to terms with bereavement, we are constantly reminded of the reality of loss by many catalysts such as the quiet house, empty chair, bed, personal objects, familiar music, and so on. Each time something is experienced for the first time without the deceased, a very strong STUG reaction may be re-triggered, but as each item or issue is faced, the associated pain is usually diminished [2, 3, 5, 17, 26]. Although a wide variety of situations can re-trigger STUG reactions, they are perhaps most commonly identified with anniversaries.

In summary, grief is clearly a universal experience, involving a non-specific set of psychological, behavioral, and physical reactions in response to the death of a significant other. It is therefore best considered to be a biopsychosocial phenomenon, incorporating biological, psychological, and social impacts on the bereaved person [8].

Various bereavement theories, different types of grief, stages of mourning, physical and social changes, and grief abnormalities, indicate that grief is not a simple, standard process, with a progression of fixed stages, each with its typical symptoms. Rather, grief has a multi-dimensional nature and a complex range of cognitive and behavioral responses.

Nevertheless, popular notions of grief involve a process of at least three phases, and concepts of normal and abnormal grief. While a common pattern is generally considered to exist, grief experiences are reported to be as individual as are the specific people experiencing the phenomenon, on the particular occasion, and under all of the given circumstances.

Successful readjustment and accommodation of grief involves working through specific tasks of the grief process. And grief may be considered pathological when normal processes of resolving the loss do not occur as anticipated.

IMPACTS OF GRIEF AND TRAUMA

Today, health is professionally considered from the more holistic, biopsychosocial perspective, with illness commonly recognized to involve a complex interaction of biological, psychological, and sociocultural factors. This is recognized by the World Health Organization, which defines health as "a state of complete physical, mental and social well-being, and not merely the absence of disease or infirmity" [27].

The distress of bereavement must also be considered within this complex model of health. Grief involves identifiable changes in emotions and thought processes, behavioral changes, interpersonal and social changes, and physical complaints [2, 26].

Manifestations of normal grief can be identified within the categories of feelings, physical sensations, cognitions, and behaviors [21].

Grief *feelings* include sadness, anger, guilt and self-reproach, anxiety, loneliness, fatigue, helplessness, shock, yearning, emancipation, relief, and numbness. *Physical sensations* include hollowness in the stomach, tightness in the chest, tightness in the throat, over-sensitivity to noise, sense of depersonalization, breathlessness, muscular weakness, lack of energy, and a dry mouth. And grief *cognitions* include disbelief, confusion, preoccupation, a sense of presence, and hallucinations [3, 5, 9, 17, 21].

Normal grief *behaviors* include sleep disturbances, appetite disturbances, absent-minded behavior, social withdrawal, dreams of the deceased, and avoiding reminders of the deceased. Other behaviors include searching and calling out, sighing, crying, visiting places or carrying objects that remind the survivor of the deceased, and treasuring objects that belonged to the deceased [5, 17, 21].

Parkes notes that bereavement involves a psychosocial transition, and that, when somebody dies, a whole set of assumptions about the world that relied upon the other person for their validity are suddenly invalidated. Habits of thought built up over many years must be reviewed and modified; a person's view of the world must change. According to Parkes, this transition inevitably takes time and effort. He considers we have been building our own model of the world since birth, and that we rely on the accuracy of these assumptions to maintain our orientation and control our lives. He concludes anything that challenges the model incapacitates us [7].

Parkes also observes that the person we would normally have turned to in times of trouble is often the person whose death is now mourned. And, therefore, when we are in the biggest trouble we have ever experienced, we may find ourselves repeatedly turning to someone who is not there [7].

The impact of bereavement on health status is profound, according to Shuchter and Zisook, who also consider that this impact extends beyond psychological to psychiatric and physical health. They found changes in functioning to include depression and anxiety, and increased consumption of alcohol, cigarettes and medications [18]. And psychoactive substance use is also reported by Rando, among what she describes as common mental disorders emanating from complicated mourning [5].

Ata found just over 3% of bereaved respondents sought psychological or psychiatric help, just under 2% were hospitalized because of the severity of their grief, but almost 24% sought medical and pharmaceutical help leading to the use of medication [10]. Ata also found coping methods to vary greatly by ethnicity of the mourner.

From a review of at least 12 studies of the effects of bereavement on health, Parkes concludes that bereavement can affect physical health, but that most of the complaints which take people to their physicians are reflections of anxiety and tension, rather than of organic disease. In such cases, he suggests that the most important role for the physician may be to reassure people that they are not sick rather than to label them as so. He does, however, agree with others, that the most extensive evidence of a link between disease in a specific organ system and bereavement exists for the cardiovascular system [2, 7]. To this he adds that certain potentially fatal conditions seem in some cases to be precipitated or aggravated by major losses.

Parkes also observes that widespread use is made of drugs to alleviate the stress of bereavement, and considers that were their popularity any indication of their value, drugs would be counted the principle treatment for grief. But, as he notes, few systematic attempts have been made to assess their effects [7].

Reaction to psychological trauma is somewhat different to that of bereavement. Traumatology is reported to be a relatively new and growing science with contributions from a multi-disciplinary basis [28]. Raphael considers psychologically traumatic stressors to be much more to do with death encounter, including personal life threat or exposure to horrific, gruesome, mutilating or other shocking death or injury [29].

Traumatic stress is experienced frequently within general communities, and as with bereavement, in most cases it does not lead to psychological or behavioral disorder [29].

However, Post Traumatic Stress Disorder (PTSD) is described as a clinical reaction to trauma, including witnessing a horrifying scene, a threat to one's own life, or a particularly traumatic bereavement [4, 5, 7, 8, 28]. This reaction involves disturbed behavior that emerges after the stressful incident is over [8]. In severe circumstances, a traumatic neurosis may block or interfere with a bereaved person's capacity to grieve [4]. In such circumstances, dealing with the trauma may be essential prior to any attempts at grief therapy. Described reactions to traumatic bereavements, such as homicide, include intrusive, vivid images of the death, nightmares, heightened arousal, hyper-vigilance, and avoidance behavior [3, 4].

Post traumatic stress disorders were first identified among U.S. Vietnam veterans in the 1970s, months after discharge from service. However, they are now recognized in response to other traumatic incidents. One study suggests that post traumatic stress disorders have been experienced by roughly 0.5% of men and 1.3% of women in the United States general population [8].

In a study of children subjected to a sniper attack, Pynoos et al. found that the magnitude of grief correlated to the intensity of attachment to a friend who had died, while the magnitude of symptoms of PTSD correlated with the extent to which the child had been in personal danger [26, 30].

Because our survival depends on our ability to learn about danger, Parkes suggests that it should not surprise us if memories of life threatening or other terrifying situations tend to persist even when the danger is past. He considers this may account for the persistence of traumatic memories that are a feature of PTSD. According to Parkes, jumpiness, hyper-alertness and irritability, fear and overreacting to non-existent dangers may seem illogical, but are part of the pattern of reaction that has enabled humans to survive in a hostile world [7].

Robinson suggests that maybe at the core of trauma is threat to life, and at the core of loss and bereavement is threat to bonding, however, there is usually some loss in trauma and some trauma in loss [28].

It may therefore be concluded that bereavement (the loss through death of a significant other) is primarily an impact of a *social* nature, and trauma (a response to severe threat or shock) is primarily an impact of a *psychological* nature. While bereavement reaction includes *separation* anxiety and a focus on the deceased, traumatic stress reaction includes *threat* anxiety and a focus on personal security.

CONCLUSION

This chapter has reviewed experiences of bereavement, and considered contemporary knowledge in the field of grief. The next chapter introduces the research methodologies employed in a quantitative cemetery Visitation Study, and a qualitative Bereavement Study.

REFERENCES

1. S. Freud, Mourning and melancholia, in *Sigmund Freud: Collected papers* (vol. 4) (J. Traviere, trans. 1959), Basic Books, New York, 1917.
2. M. Osterweis, F. Solomon, and M. Green (eds.), *Bereavement: Reactions, consequences, and care*, National Academy Press, Washington, D.C., 1984.
3. B. Raphael, *The anatomy of bereavement: A handbook for the caring professions*, Routledge, London, 1984.
4. W. Middleton, B. Raphael, N. Martinek, and V. Misso, Pathological grief reactions, in *Handbook of bereavement: Theory, research, and intervention*, M. S. Stroebe, W. Stroebe, and R. O. Hansson (eds.), Cambridge University Press, Cambridge, 1993.
5. T. A. Rando, *Treatment of complicated mourning*, Research Press, Champaign, Illinois, 1993.
6. J. Bowlby, The making and breaking of affectional bonds: I: Aetiology and psychopathology in the light of attachment theory (the fiftieth Maudsley Lecture), *The British Journal of Psychiatry, 130*, pp. 201-210, 1977.
7. C. M. Parkes, *Bereavement: Studies of grief in adult life* (3rd ed.), Penguin, London, 1996.
8. W. Weiten, *Psychology: Themes and variations* (4th ed.), Brooks/Cole, Pacific Grove, California, 1998.
9. Attig, T., *How we grieve: Relearning the world*, Oxford University Press, New York, 1996.
10. A. W. Ata, *Bereavement & health in Australia: Gender, psychological, religious and cross-cultural issues*, David Lovell, Melbourne, 1994.
11. E. Lindemann, Symptomatology and management of acute grief, *American Journal of Psychiatry, 101*, pp. 141-148, 1944.

12. G. E. Westberg, *Good grief: A constructive approach to the problem of loss*, Joint Board of Christian Education, Melbourne, 1992.
13. J. Bowlby, Processes of mourning, *International Journal of Psychoanalysis, 42,* pp. 317-340, 1961.
14. G. Engel, Grief and grieving, *American Journal of Nursing, 64,* pp. 93-98, 1964.
15. E. Kübler-Ross, *On death and dying,* Tavistock, London (also Macmillan, New York), 1969.
16. C. M. Parkes, Seeking and finding a lost object: Evidence from recent studies of the reaction to bereavement, in *Normal and pathological responses to bereavement,* MSS Information Corporation, New York, 1974.
17. C. M. Sanders, *Grief: The mourning after, dealing with adult bereavement*, Wiley Interscience, New York, 1989.
18. S. R. Shuchter and S. Zisook, The course of normal grief, in *Handbook of bereavement: Theory, research, and intervention,* M. S. Stroebe, W. Stroebe, and R. O. Hansson (eds.), Cambridge University Press, Cambridge, 1993.
19. J. A. Walter, *The revival of death,* Routledge, London, 1994.
20. P. Bachelor, *Cemetery visitation: The place of the cemetery in the grief process,* unpublished Ph.D. thesis, Charles Sturt University, Wagga Wagga, 2001.
21. J. W. Worden, *Grief counselling and grief therapy: A handbook for the mental health practitioner* (2nd ed.), Routledge, London, 1991.
22. R. S. Weiss, Loss and recovery, in *Handbook of bereavement: Theory, research, and intervention,* M. S. Stroebe, W. Stroebe, and R. O. Hansson (eds.), Cambridge University Press, Cambridge, 1993.
23. D. Klass, Elisabeth Kübler-Ross and the tradition of the private sphere, *Omega, 12*(3), pp. 241-265, 1981.
24. N. O'Connor, *Letting go with love: The grieving process*, La Mariposa, Arizona, 1986.
25. E. N. Jackson, Grief, in *Concerning death: A practical guide for the living,* E. A. Grollman (ed.), Beacon Press, Boston, 1974.
26. M. S. Stroebe, W. Stroebe, and R. O. Hansson (eds.), *Handbook of bereavement: Theory, research, and intervention*, Cambridge University Press, Cambridge, 1993.
27. Australian Bureau of Statistics, *2003 Year book Australia*, Cat. No. 1301.0, A.G.P.S., Canberra, 2003.
28. R. Robinson, Finding the trauma in loss and the loss in trauma, *Grief Matters: The Australian Journal of Grief and Bereavement, 2*(2), pp. 25-28, 1999.
29. B. Raphael, Trauma and grief, *Grief Matters: The Australian Journal of Grief and Bereavement, 2*(2), pp. 22-24, 1999.
30. R. S. Pynoos, C. Frederick, K. Nader, W. Arroyo, A. Steinberg, S. Eth, F. Nunez, and L. Fairbanks, Life threat and post-traumatic reactions in school-age children, *Archives of General Psychiatry, 44,* pp. 1057-1063, 1987.

CHAPTER 4

Research Methodologies

The previous chapter reviewed experiences of bereavement, and considered contemporary wisdom in the field of grief. Now, in concluding Part A on the background to the cemetery Visitation and Bereavement Studies, this chapter discusses the research methodologies employed in these recent studies.

Over the past 15 years, I have undertaken several specific cemetery visitation studies. However, most of the data to be presented in Parts B and C is drawn from two major research projects. The first was a quantitative demographic study of cemetery visitation throughout Australia, to which I refer as the Visitation Study. The second was a qualitative ethnographic study of recently bereaved persons, to which I refer as the Bereavement Study. To a lesser extent, I also engaged in naturalistic observations of cemetery visitors.

In recognizing the inevitability of some limitations with any behavioral research, Parkes commends the complementary values of quantitative and qualitative bereavement research, toward maximizing the value of findings [1].

> We shall never be able to fully understand any piece of human behavior, nor can we expect to identify major factors that are important to outcomes in every case of bereavement. But we can, I believe, learn something of the factors that play a part in most cases and a major part in some.

> Relevant data can be obtained from detailed studies of a few people or from statistical studies of larger samples. Ideally, the two types of study should compliment each other, for it is only by studying large numbers of people that we can generalize, and only by intensively studying a few that we can evaluate the significance of the mathematics of many [1, p. 118].

Sociology offers systematic and objective investigation of the social world, using a range of rigorous methodological standards, techniques, and practices. As with any other skilled work, an initial challenge of the researcher is to select and apply the most appropriate tools to the task at hand.

A general exploration of the social phenomenon of cemetery visitation best suited a quantitative approach, and this certainly provided a very revealing overview of this previously little-known human behavior. However, the trouble with generalizations is that they don't apply to particulars [2]. So, to complement and expand my initial quantitative findings, further qualitative investigation was undertaken to identify and interpret personal meanings of cemetery visitation from the perspectives of the social actors themselves.

The Visitation Study employed a highly structured, quantitative questionnaire to obtain answers to specific questions, and the Bereavement Study involved a series of semi-structured, in-depth interviews to reveal qualitative personal experiences. Naturalistic observations included unobtrusively observing the natural behaviors of cemetery visitors, and recording the quantities of visitors of each sex visiting graves and memorials, the durations of such visits, and the quantities of mourners participating in funerals.

Quantitative and qualitative approaches to sociological research are well regarded to be complementary and it is noted that many researchers combine elements from both methods in specific research projects [3]. This was also my approach toward maximizing our understanding of the sociocultural phenomenon of cemetery visitation.

QUANTITATIVE METHODOLOGY

During 1997 to 1998, I coordinated visitor surveys at 13 prominent general cemeteries, which collectively facilitated 28% of all Australian burials and cremations, and hosted almost 8.5 million annual visits. For each participating cemetery, the studies offered an opportunity to identify numbers and visitation patterns, key social and cultural demographics, and issues of particular note to their specific but diverse clients.

A standard questionnaire was devised to obtain directly comparable responses from visitors at each cemetery. Data obtained from the survey questions included a specific primary bereavement (and grave or memorial) to which other data relates, the perceived nationality and religion of the family of the decedent, and the primary service choice (burial or cremation). It also included the usual frequency of visits, incidence of personal anniversary visits, period since the respective death, and the age and sex of the visitor. The opportunity was also taken to obtain limited qualitative data on significant service issues that particularly satisfy and dissatisfy visitors to the respective cemetery.

At each participating cemetery, randomized samples of either 200 or 300 visitors were interviewed, comprising a total sample of 3,000 visitors. Generally, data collection occurred with vehicles and/or pedestrians randomly stopped as they entered the site. At all cemeteries, visitor samples were drawn throughout the week.

The privacy of any visitors who did not wish to be interviewed was fully respected. However, in all cemeteries only very small proportions (2% to 5%) declined. Most mourners were very happy to talk, and appreciated the opportunity to express themselves to someone prepared to listen to what was most important to them. While these interviews averaged 10 minutes duration, it often became necessary to truncate further discussion after 30 or so minutes.

Appropriate traffic survey methods were also employed to identify the numbers of people, in and out of vehicles, entering the premises on each day of the week.

Other data acquired from each cemetery included the numbers of burial and cremation services conducted each day of the week, and the average numbers of mourners attending graveside and/or crematorium services.

The research was supervised and conducted in association with Charles Sturt University's Johnstone Centre for Social and Biophysical Environmental Research, and its trustworthiness measured in terms of internal and external validity, reliability, and objectivity.

NATURALISTIC OBSERVATION

Naturalistic observation involves the observation of behavior without direct intervention. This method was specifically utilized in one relatively small, but nonetheless important study, because it was considered a more reliable method of identifying durations of visits to specific cemetery compartments than relying on the accuracy of self-reporting.

Durations of cemetery visits were extrapolated from observations made at each of several specific cemetery compartments at Australia's largest and busiest cemetery (with around 2.25 million visits per year). Random visits (involving one or more visitors) were observed throughout a week during winter and, for comparison, also during summer. As no clear variation by season was discernible, the data were then combined for further analysis. The specific cemetery compartments surveyed for this study included a mausoleum, a Catholic monumental section, an Orthodox monumental section, a general lawn grave area, a general memorial garden area, and a general children's lawn grave area.

Recorded observations included the number and sex of persons in each group, and the corresponding interval between arrival at the grave or memorial site and departure of the visitors.

QUALITATIVE METHODOLOGY

While a conventional quantitative approach best suited the initial exploratory investigation of the generalities of cemetery visitation, adequate sociological description of various personal values of the cemetery within contexts of grief required a qualitative study to reveal individual meanings of observable behavior.

So, for the Bereavement Study, an interpretive social science, ethnographic case study approach was considered appropriate within a naturalistic or qualitative perspective of inquiry.

The interpretive paradigm suggests that everyone does not share the same meaning system or hold the same values, but rather, each person's perception becomes their own reality. Rather than seeing things as *they* are, we are more likely to see things as *we* are. Social, physical and intellectual realities can change for individuals over time, and in response to specific events. As Craib puts it, we understand people when we understand what they think they know about the world, their meanings, and self-conceptions [4].

Naturalistic research is so called because behavior is allowed to unfold naturally, or without interference, in its natural environment; that is, within the setting in which it would normally occur [5]. Naturalistic inquiry employs qualitative methodology in attempting to understand individual values of a specific social phenomenon from the perspective of the social actors.

With the Bereavement Study, in-depth interviews were the primary source of data collection. And since the quantitative data had already indicated relationship of the decedent and religion of the family to be the more significant determinants of cemetery visitation, purposive sampling was employed to obtain a good cross-section of these variables in particular.

Neuman suggests that purposive sampling is appropriate in three situations: to select unique cases that are especially informative, to select members of a difficult to reach, specialized population, and to identify particular types of cases for in-depth investigation [3]. All three situations for purposive sampling presented themselves in the qualitative Bereavement Study.

In naturalistic studies, purposive sampling offers advantages over generalization-oriented random sampling, which Lincoln and Guba suggest, is likely to suppress more deviant cases, as well as the likelihood that a full array of multiple realities will be uncovered [2].

> Naturalistic sampling . . . is based on informational, not statistical, considerations. Its purpose is to maximize information, not facilitate generalization. . . . the criterion invoked to determine when to stop sampling is informational redundancy, not a statistical confidence level [2, p. 202].

Though the cases were intended to represent the specific experiences of a few individuals only, informants were purposively selected to include common attributes of typical cemetery visitors, as identified from the qualitative data. These attributes are of the variables: religion, relationship, nationality, primary service, age, and sex.

Qualitative data analysis was inductive. Inductive data analysis begins with detailed observations of the world and moves toward more abstract generalizations and ideas, rather than from pre-existing theories or hypotheses. As Lincoln and Guba say, it is the inverse of the usual mode of deductive data analysis used in conventional quantitative investigations [2]. Naturalistic investigation typically does not work with either a priori theory or variables (both being characteristics of conventional studies); these are expected to emerge from the inquiry.

Interviews were generally conducted where informants felt most comfortable. Most occurred in private homes, some took place within the offices of a large general cemetery, and some in a hotel suite.

The research involved no coercion, deception, or invasion of privacy. All informants were fully informed and each acknowledged that the data collection process might evoke emotions of loss and grief. With some emotional releases, pauses of respite did occur, though no informants chose to cease interviews, even when specifically reminded of that option. The interviews were all tape-recorded, and the confidentiality of data and anonymity of the informants were guaranteed.

Each person interviewed formally consented to his or her story being recorded. In each case, the presence of a tape recorder was quickly ignored and so did not impede natural flow of conversation. Questions were kept to a minimum, and simply served as a guide to ensure that comparable information was obtained in each case.

Most interviews involved one-on-one discussions between a single mourner and myself, though three married couples participated, and three individuals had the comfort of a close friend or family member present. In another two cases, the daughters of non-English-speaking widows assisted with language interpretation.

The main interviews ranged in duration from less than one hour to over three hours. Some participants were quite composed, objective, and pragmatic, while other interviews involved highly emotional outpourings.

In several cases, home visits included guided tours to show me how the mourners now live, and to see photographs and other memorabilia of the deceased. Wherever possible, I also visited respective cemeteries, graves, and memorials, to gain additional personal insights into individual scenes of funerals and commemorative visitation.

A transcript was made of each tape recording and these were then edited, deleting unnecessary or irrelevant discussion, including my own questions and any superfluous repetitions. To ensure anonymity of interviewees, their real names, several places and organizations, and some other identifying factors were changed. Some broken speech was reconstructed where this enhanced clarity of expression. In each case, editing resulted in a condensed draft case study report.

These draft reports were then presented to respective mourners, or their representatives, to validate accurate portrayal of expressed words and feelings. Participants were asked to suggest any corrections, additions, or deletions to their respective case study. Most were completely satisfied with the first draft. Only two interviewees requested minor alterations: one to correct a technicality of detail, and the other to improve some word selection.

The following comments were typical verbatim responses to the draft case studies:

> There's nothing I would change. I mean, that's what I said. It's just my words.
>> *40-year-old Italian Catholic son*

> It's very accurate. I thought it was very good. My daughter also read it and she also thought it was very good.
>> *66-year-old Maltese Catholic husband*

> It was really funny reading what I said. My husband also had a laugh, because he read it too. I said, "Do I really sound like that?" And he said, "That's exactly you; that's just how you sound."
>> *35-year-old Australian*
>> *non-religious granddaughter*

Much more so than with the brief quantitative survey interviews, these qualitative in-depth interviews allowed informants to review their own situations and consider their responses. Some informants had previously related very little, if any, detail of their personal experiences to anyone else, and had not clarified their perspectives of grief for themselves. In several such cases, participants or their partners reported that the respective interview experience and draft case study review had provided some cathartic value.

> The interview reads well and is as [my friend] spoke, so we both agreed that it reflects accurately how he responded to your questions. I must tell you that after the actual interview, [he] was surprised at how much he had been able to feel again and welcomed the opportunity. It was very therapeutic for him.
>> *Companion of 51-year-old Australian non-religious husband*

> It was really helpful to read what you wrote. I got the feeling you really understood how we felt. It was really interesting to read what we went through; and I think it's helped me somehow to get over it more.
>> *60-year-old Australian non-religious grandmother*

Other researchers have found similar responses. As Parkes says:

> The very act of persuading the bereaved person to explain their situation to an ignorant outsider can be very therapeutic for, while the other person is explaining themselves to us, they are also explaining themselves to themselves and getting the situation into perspective [1, p. 184].

The qualitative data collection and its analysis for the Bereavement Study proved to be much more emotionally taxing than was the preceding quantitative Visitation Study. This was also to be expected, as the high psychological, social, and physical costs of fieldwork have been well recognized by other social researchers [3, 6].

This research was also supervised and conducted in association with Charles Sturt University's Johnstone Centre for Social and Biophysical Environmental

Research, and its trustworthiness was measured in terms of Lincoln and Guba's naturalistic research trustworthiness criteria: credibility, transferability, dependability, and confirmability [2].

CONCLUSION

This discussion of research methodologies now concludes Part A, which is presented to establish a suitable background to the Visitation Study and Bereavement Study. Part B now looks at key findings of the Visitation Study, and in particular, identifies general patterns of visitation and significant social and cultural influences on visitation.

REFERENCES

1. C. M. Parkes, *Bereavement: Studies of grief in adult life* (3rd ed.), Penguin, London, 1996.
2. Y. S. Lincoln and E. G. Guba, *Naturalistic inquiry,* Sage, California, 1985.
3. W. L. Neuman, *Social research methods: Qualitative and quantitative approaches* (3rd ed.), Allyn & Bacon, Boston, 1997.
4. I. Craib, *Modern social theory: From Parsons to Habermas* (2nd ed.), Harvester Wheatsheaf, London, 1992.
5. W. Weiten, *Psychology: Themes and variations* (4th ed.), Brooks/Cole, Pacific Grove, California, 1998.
6. R. Bogdan and S. J. Taylor, *Introduction to qualitative research methods: A phenomenological approach to the social sciences,* Wiley, New York, 1975.

Part B

In Part A we reviewed the evolution of the modern cemetery environment, looked at contemporary death, current concepts of bereavement and grief, and the methodologies employed in both the Visitation and Bereavement Studies. This established a background context for the quantitative research findings presented in this part, and also for the qualitative findings to be presented in Part C.

Part B now presents major findings of the quantitative Visitation Study, identifies the volume of visits, common visitation patterns, and the significance of common social and cultural attributes within cemetery visitation.

CHAPTER 5
Visitation Patterns

This chapter reviews the volume of visits to what appear to be modern society's most significant cultural sites. Common patterns of visitation behavior are here identified, considering several factors, including frequency, duration, anniversary visits, and a long-term visitation trajectory.

SIGNIFICANCE OF CEMETERY VISITATION

Urban memorial parks are among the most visited places in modern communities. They are virtual hives of activity with recently bereaved persons of diverse cultural backgrounds. Within Australia, more than 1.5 visits per head of the national population occur within cemeteries each year. Some larger cemeteries, hosting literally millions of annual visits, are evidently more frequented than many major tourist attractions.

While cemeteries are often considered simply as places for the disposition of human remains, the main, ongoing use of what are arguably our most significant cultural sites is actually for subsequent memorial visitation. The Visitation Study revealed that 77% of cemetery traffic relates to commemorative visits, and funeral corteges were found to represent the remaining 23%.

In reviewing urban parks and their visitors, Hamilton-Smith and Mercer note that wild-land and national parks have been subject to literally many thousands of research studies, and that we consequently have a considerable understanding of the issues in such areas. But, as they note, there has been little similar research on urban parks, which they consider a much more difficult and complex topic [1].

Drawing on over 25 years experience in managing urban and provincial parks systems, I suggest that within the category of urban parks lies an even *more* difficult and complex topic—that of *memorial parks*. The utility of these places is not merely recreational for some people, but practical, spiritual, and cultural, and for all members of our communities at the most difficult time in their lives.

Their use is not casual, but of high intensity and deep personal significance. And until the recent Visitation Study and Bereavement Study, social-behavioral research within cemeteries and memorial parks had not even been attempted.

With the volume of visits made to these places each year, the roles of our cemeteries and the values of memorial visitation have clearly been significant omissions from social behavioral studies and existing bereavement literature. For literally hundreds of millions of bereaved persons of various social and cultural backgrounds, this most important bereavement behavioral activity is a crucial component of satisfactorily working through their personal grief.

PATTERNS

General patterns of cemetery visitation reflect several factors, including the mourner's frequency and duration of visits, their relative position on a long-term visitation trajectory, and the incidence of special occasion visits. This section reviews these factors, and discusses when and for how long mourners typically visit cemeteries.

The Visitation Study revealed different frequencies of visitation to be most evident by duration of bereavement, relationship to the decedent, family ethnicity, and service type (a choice relating to ethnicity). Those found most likely to visit a cemetery at least once each week include people attending the grave of their own child, spouse, or parent, those of Greek-Orthodox and Italian-Catholic families, and those visiting a grave rather than a cremation memorial. Conversely, those found most likely to make very-infrequent visits to a cemetery include people attending the grave of a grandparent or friend, those of Protestant and non-religious families, those of British and Australian families, and those visiting a cremation memorial rather than a grave.

The mean duration of cemetery visits was found to be just over 24 minutes, but duration does vary significantly by social and cultural factors, particularly the visitor's emotional attachment to the decedent, ethnicity of the family, and sex of the visitor. Many more females than males visit cemeteries in the first place, and observations at Australia's most visited cemetery revealed the mean duration of visits by females to be greater than the mean duration of visits by males to each one of several culturally diverse cemetery compartments.

Personal anniversaries, which mainly related to the death and birthday of the decedent, were found to precipitate one in every five visits to cemeteries.

The study showed that the vast majority of cemetery visits occur within a relatively short interval of the respective death, and the typical wane in visitation follows a similar pattern among persons of various social and cultural backgrounds. As no significant variation from the general trend was found to be unique to any specific social or cultural identity, I propose that the typical long-term visitation trajectory (Figure 5.5, p. 55) may be a universal phenomenon. Further support for this idea comes from the reports of most participants in the

Bereavement Study who correlated waning cemetery visitation to subsidence in their emotions of grief.

FREQUENCY

In the Visitation Study, the majority of cemetery visits were found to follow regular patterns, as shown in Figure 5.1, with the most popular frequency being weekly. In fact, just over 41% of the sample 3,000 visitors were found to visit *at least* once each week (i.e., Daily to Weekly) [2].

Visitor activity was found to generally follow clearly defined regular patterns with no significant seasonal variation, other than slightly shorter stays during unpleasant weather. Figure 5.2 shows the mean proportions of weekly cemetery traffic, including the funeral component, occurring each day throughout a normal week.

Funeral corteges were found to comprise some 23% of the total weekly traffic volume, with the bulk of visits representing memorial visitation. Evidently, the most popular days for commemorative visits are the weekend days of Friday, Saturday, and Sunday.

The greater incidence of funeral traffic on Fridays relates to pre-weekend funerals for those who die mid-week. The next highest incidence of funeral traffic, on Wednesdays, and lowest on Mondays, reflects time required to plan and publicize funerals for those who die on weekends.

The very low incidences of funeral traffic on Saturdays and virtual absence on Sundays reflects the influence of prevailing Christian traditions, including a

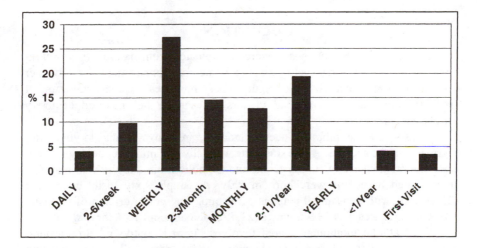

Figure 5.1 Frequencies of all visits.
Source: Bachelor [3].

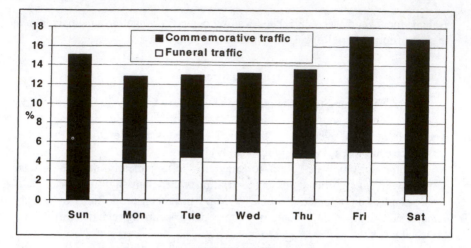

Figure 5.2 Mean vehicles over a normal week
Source: Bachelor [3].

reluctance to request funerals on weekends (especially Sundays) and the reluctance of many cemeteries, funeral directors, clergy, and others to provide such services outside the customary business week of Monday to Friday.

The mean number of mourners attending graveside or crematorium services at all cemeteries was found to be 51. More, or in some cases fewer, people may have attended a preceding service at a church or funeral parlor.

DURATION

Durations of cemetery visits were extrapolated from naturalistic observations made of visits to several specific cemetery compartments at Fawkner Crematorium & Memorial Park. Figure 5.3 summarizes the mean duration of visits by females, males, and all visitors to each of the specified cemetery compartments.

Mausoleum entombment occurs indoors, in above-ground crypts with engraved granite shutters. At the study site, virtually all families choosing mausoleum entombment are of Italian origin and Catholic faith, and the vast majority of encrypted decedents were born in Italy. A sample sixty visits comprised 121 visitors, with a mean 2.0 persons per group. The mean duration of all visits to this specific area was 18.9 minutes (21.5 for females and 15.4 for males).

The Catholic monumental area involves burial in outdoor below-ground concrete vaults with full monumental cover. The majority of all families burying in the Catholic monumental area at the study site are also of Italian origin. A sample sixty visits comprised 129 visitors, with a mean 2.1 persons per group. The

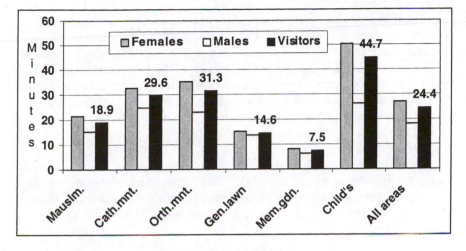

Figure 5.3 Mean duration of visits to specified cemetery compartments.
Source: Bachelor [3].

mean duration of all visits to this specific area was 29.6 minutes (32.6 for females and 25.0 for males).

The Orthodox monumental area involves burial in earthen graves with full monumental cover. Most Orthodox visitors at the study site are of Greek families, though several other eastern European nationalities are less well represented. A sample sixty visits comprised 113 visitors, with a mean 1.9 persons per group. The mean duration of all visits to this specific area was 31.3 minutes (35.3 for females and 22.8 for males).

The general lawn area involves burial in earthen graves with lawn cover and flush bronze plaques. General lawn areas at the study site are utilized by diverse families, but are particularly popular among those of Anglo background. A sample sixty visits comprised 104 visitors, with a mean 1.8 persons per group. The mean duration of all visits to this specific area was 14.6 minutes (15.3 for females and 13.7 for males).

The memorial garden involves cremated remains interred in a variety of garden and wall-niches with small bronze plaques. Memorial gardens are utilized by families of diverse backgrounds, but at the study site are more popular among Anglo-Protestant and non-religious families. A sample sixty visits comprised 99 visitors, with a mean 1.6 persons per group. The mean duration of all visits to this specific area was 7.5 minutes (8.0 for females and 6.4 for males).

The children's lawn area involves burial in earthen graves with lawn cover and a choice of raised bronze plaques or small monuments. Burial in this area is restricted to those under 13 years of age. A sample sixty visits comprised 108 visitors, with a mean 1.8 persons per group. The mean duration of all visits to this specific area was 44.7 minutes (50.2 for females and 26.3 for males).

So, the mean duration of female visits was found to be greater than that of male visits in each of six specific cemetery compartments frequented by various cultural and social groups. To all compartments combined, mean visits by females were found to be 49.5% longer than mean visits by males (i.e., 27.2 and 18.2 minutes respectively). The greatest variation occurred among visits to children's graves, where mean visits by females were found to be 90.8% longer than mean visits by males.

Females were also found much less likely than males to visit adult graves alone, but mothers were much more likely than fathers to make solo visits to their children's graves, and widows were more likely than widowers to visit memorial gardens (involving cremation memorials) on their own.

ANNIVERSARIES

The Visitation Study identified that of all cemetery visits, virtually 20% coincide with a personal anniversary, as shown in Figure 5.4. This highlights the apparent significance of anniversaries, particularly of death and birthday, in precipitating visits.

Other anniversaries in the sample included Hellenic name days and personal occasions such as "anniversary of our first date."

As well as these personal anniversaries, certain public anniversaries, such as Mothers Day, Fathers Day, and religious festivals, including Christmas and

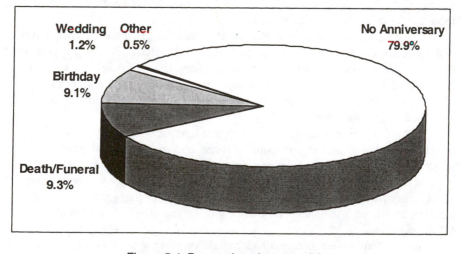

Figure 5.4 Personal anniversary visits.
Source: Bachelor [3].

Easter, can also be very important occasions to visit the cemetery. Specific cultural groups observe other anniversaries, so that increased visits to certain areas may also be anticipated. Other notable occasions of specific cultural importance include Orthodox Christmas, Orthodox Easter, All Saints and All Souls Days, and the Islamic feasts *Eidul Fitr* and *Eidul Adha*.

Memorial plaques or inscriptions, commonly bearing dates of birth and death, can thereby indicate likely dates of subsequent visits to the cemetery. And noting these dates can be of significant management value toward minimizing family distress, when planning works in the vicinity of a specific grave or memorial.

TRAJECTORY

Visiting a memorial is evidently of greater personal value to those who are recently bereaved and still working through intense grief. As mourners gradually adjust to bereavement, grief intensity subsides and the personal need to visit a memorial correspondingly diminishes.

A typical visitation trajectory was constructed from data relating to the 3,000 visitors in the Visitation Study. Figure 5.5 shows the proportions of cemetery visitors attending each year since the death of a significant other. The data indicate that 21% of all cemetery visits occur within one year of the respective death. Only 5.2% of all visits occur five years after a death, just 2.5% ten years after, 1% fifteen years after the death, and only 0.7% twenty years after. The median interval between death and a cemetery visit was found to be 3.7 years.

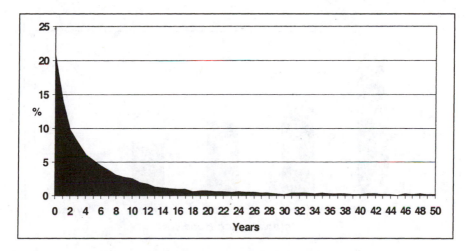

Figure 5.5 Cemetery visitation trajectory.
Source: Bachelor [3].

Figure 5.5 illustrates the typical fluid transition from intense regular visitation shortly after a funeral, to very infrequent, periodical, and perhaps even casual visitation years later. I suggest this also graphically depicts the corresponding subsidence in intensity of grief reported by the majority of mourners in the Bereavement Study. While this subsidence is initially dramatic and most mourners progressively overcome the severe impacts of a significant loss, the fact of loss remains for the life of the survivor.

Placing flowers was identified in the Bereavement Study as the most common activity of most cemetery visitors. So the proportion of graves, in given areas of known ages, found to be bearing flowers may be taken as a further indication of the level of visitation to these graves.

A review of general lawn graves at Fawkner Memorial Park revealed fresh flowers on 35% of those where a burial had been conducted up to a month earlier. Of similar graves where burial had occurred up to a year earlier, the proportion of fresh flowers was 25%. This reduced to 18% at up to two years, 13% at up to three years, and 9% at up to four years, as shown in Figure 5.6.

SUMMARY

Different frequencies of general cemetery visitation are most evident by the duration of bereavement, relationship to the decedent, family ethnicity, and service type. Those found most likely to visit a cemetery at least once each week include people attending the grave of their own child, spouse, or parent, those of Greek-Orthodox and Italian-Catholic families, and those visiting a grave

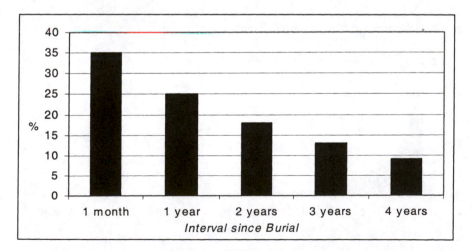

Figure 5.6 Proportions of graves bearing flowers up to four years from burial.
Source: Bachelor [3].

rather than a cremation memorial. Conversely, those found most likely to make very-infrequent visits to a cemetery include people attending the grave of a grandparent or friend, those of Protestant and non-religious families, those of British and Australian families, and those visiting a cremation memorial rather than a grave.

The mean duration of all commemorative visits was found to be just over 24 minutes. However, the specific duration varies significantly by social and cultural factors, and appears most closely related to the visitor's emotional bond to the decedent, ethnicity of the family, and sex of the visitor. Many more females than males visit cemeteries, and the mean duration of visits by females was found to be greater than the mean duration of visits by males.

The vast majority of cemetery visits occur within a relatively short interval of the respective death, and the typical wane of cemetery visitation follows a similar pattern among persons of various social and cultural backgrounds.

Having now considered the volume of visits and identified common patterns of visitation behavior, the next chapter examines major social determinants of cemetery visitation.

REFERENCES

1. E. Hamilton-Smith and D. Mercer, *Urban parks and their visitors,* Melbourne and Metropolitan Board of Works, Victoria, 1991.
2. P. Bachelor, *Cemetery Visitors in Australia,* Eleventh National Conference of the Australian Cemeteries & Crematoria Association, Alice Springs, August 30-September 3, 1998.
3. P. Bachelor, *Cemetery visitation: The place of the cemetery in the grief process,* unpublished Ph.D. thesis, Charles Sturt University, Wagga Wagga, 2001.

CHAPTER 6
Social Factors

The cemetery is indeed a highly social environment. Having discussed the volume of visits and common visitation patterns in the previous chapter, this chapter now looks at social determinants of cemetery visitation, including the relationship of the decedent, and age and sex of the visitor.

There exists a greater likelihood of cemetery visitation where a high degree of pre-morbid emotional attachment to the decedent existed. A greater total *volume* of visits is made to graves or memorials of parents, while graves or memorials of spouses and children receive a greater degree of more *frequent* visits.

Three types of bereavement are reported to cause inordinate grief: the deaths of a child, spouse, and parent [1-3]. These are the same relationships to which the Visitation Study found virtually 80% of all cemetery visits relate, and to which virtually 90% of more frequent visits (i.e., at least once per week) are made. This correlation, and the qualitative data, link the frequency of cemetery visitation to the degree of emotional attachment or dependence on the decedent, implicating cemetery visitation as a most significant aspect of working through grief for many mourners.

As the vast majority of cemetery visitation relates to loss of a close relative, and the incidence of such loss typically increases as we progress through life, cemetery visitors are naturally older than the general population. The median age of Australian cemetery visitors was found to be over 20 years greater than that of the general population.

Females are much more inclined to visit the cemetery than are males, and not just because they commonly outlive their spouses.

RELATIONSHIP

The Visitation Study revealed that just over 95% of cemetery visits specifically involve attending the grave or memorial of a relative, and almost all other visits are to graves of close friends. Figure 6.1 indicates the proportions of visitors by relationship of the decedent to the visitor.

The most significant group of cemetery visitors, by relationship of the decedent, is those visiting a parent's memorial (38%), followed by those visiting that of a late spouse (30%). Of course, more visitors have a deceased parent than most other relationships, with the obvious exception of grandparent, but the general devotion to visiting the memorial of a grandparent (6%) is evidently much less than toward that of a parent. Considering that fewer people have a deceased spouse or child, the incidence of visits to these relations is also indicative of very strong emotional bonds.

The category *Other*, in Figure 6.1, identifies the proportion of visitors attending for reasons other than to attend the grave or memorial of a relative or friend. These visits were just less than 0.1% recreational, and just over 0.1% history and heritage related. So while much may be heard of promulgated heritage and leisure values of cemeteries, the incidence of actual community use for such purposes (at no more than two per thousand visitors combined) is evidently minuscule relative to the values of commemorative visitation.

No significant variation from the general visitation trajectory (Figure 5.5, p. 55) is evident by relationship of the decedent, as illustrated in Figure 6.2. However, significant variation in the frequency of visits is evident by relationship of the decedent, as shown in Figure 6.3. To enable direct comparison between the specific frequencies for each relationship, proportions expressed in Figures 6.2 and 6.3 are of the respective relationship, rather than of total visitors.

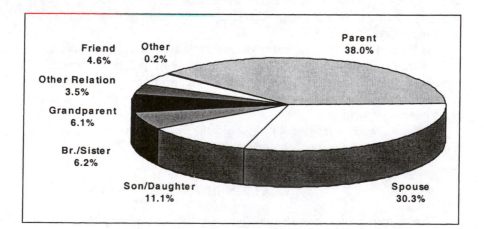

Figure 6.1 Proportions of visitors by relationship of decedent.
Source: Bachelor [4].

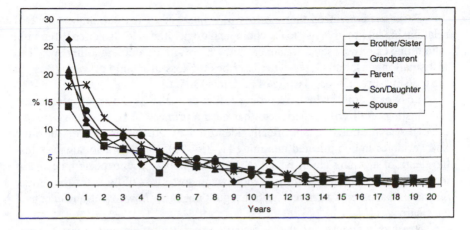

Figure 6.2 Proportions of visitors each year since death by relationship of decedent. **Source:** Bachelor [4].

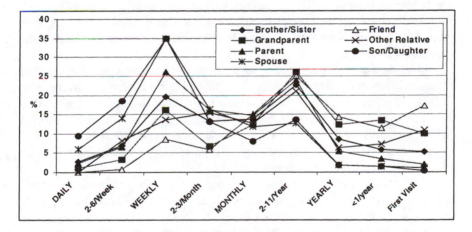

Figure 6.3 Proportions of visits at specific frequencies by relationship of the decedent. **Source:** Bachelor [4].

Higher proportions of visits occur to the memorials of spouses and children among the greater frequencies, while visits to grandparents, other relations and friends are represented more among the lesser frequencies. Of all mourners visiting a son or daughter's grave or memorial, almost 63% reported that they do so *at least* once a week (i.e., Daily to Weekly). Of those visiting a spouse's memorial, almost 55% report that they visit *at least* once each week, while among those visiting a parent's memorial, almost 35% report the same frequency.

Parkes is convinced that the loss of a husband is the commonest type of relationship loss to give rise to psychological difficulties. He also cites Wretmark, who found extremely severe and incapacitating reactions among mothers who had lost small infants, and Gorer, who describes the loss of a child at any age as the most distressing and long-lasting of all griefs [3, 5, 6].

Loss of a child, which according to Sanders also is the most intense and long-lasting of all grief experiences, has been a primary focus of much bereavement research, and it is specifically identified by Rando as one of the high risk variables in complicated mourning [1, 2, 7-10]. Raphael also suggests that the death of a young child, which is often complex and unexpected, seems to represent some failure of family or society and some loss of hope for the future. She notes that parents often feel irrational guilt no matter how loving and adequate their care was [1].

Death of a spouse has also attracted a great deal of research interest, with more work conducted on widows as they are found to be both more inclined to retain their widow status longer and more willing to participate in such studies [1-3, 8, 9]. From comparative studies, Parkes concluded that both American and British widows generally react to bereavement in a similar manner [3].

As Raphael points out, death threatens the family unit as well as each individual member. Necessary adjustments within the family system include shifts in personal roles [1].

Over the past two decades I have been directly involved with hundreds of particularly difficult cemetery clients, exhibiting complex unresolved grief issues. My own experience suggests the most common relationships of the deceased to these mourners are children (with the mode of death commonly illness or accident) and young adults (with the mode of death commonly motor accident or suicide). In these cases, whole families are tragically plunged into trauma with little or no time for comprehension or adjustment.

The loss of a father is another significant factor among difficult mourners, and I have found this particularly apparent among middle-aged Italian men, where a dramatic family role transition (to head of the family at its time of greatest crisis) may be an essential part of their personal upheaval. I have also found unsettled family disputes, including previous ambivalence or animosity toward the decedent (with no opportunity now for personal resolution) to be an issue with other difficult mourners.

A supportive family structure is evidently an important factor toward a satisfactory bereavement outcome; and in general, it seems that marriage provides some protection from the traumatic effects of the death of parents [3].

AGE

The Visitation Study revealed how the age of cemetery visitors reflects their stage in the life cycle and the incidence of death among the more frequently visited relationships. In fact the median age of cemetery visitors was found to be 56 years, which was over 20 years older than the general population average.

Figure 6.4 shows the proportions of visitors within age decade intervals, and how these compare with those of the general population [11]. The low incidence of visitors under forty years of age clearly represents a significant variance from the general population.

For both cultural and social reasons, comparatively few children visit cemeteries. Mourners of many cultural backgrounds tend not to take children to cemeteries, and much fewer young people have experienced a close bereavement than generally occurs during mid and later life.

As a person progresses through the life cycle, the incidence of death among close family members (especially parents and spouses) increases their reasons to visit. However, in the latter stages of life, visitation may be truncated by the mourner's lower ability to attend, and their own eventual demise.

Figures 6.5 and 6.6 show that no significant variations occur by age from the general visitation trajectory (Figure 5.5, p. 55), or in the general frequencies of visits (Figure 5.1, p. 51). While age may be a major determinant of cemetery visitation, it does not appear to be a significant factor in influencing specific patterns within visitation.

The median age of visitors varies by relationship to the decedent, as shown in Table 6.1. It is apparent that as a person progresses through his/her adult life, a shift typically occurs in the prime relation visited at the cemetery, starting with a grandparent and progressing ultimately to spouse.

Implications of the older median age of cemetery visitors include the need for consideration of special requirements of the aged in planning and cemetery

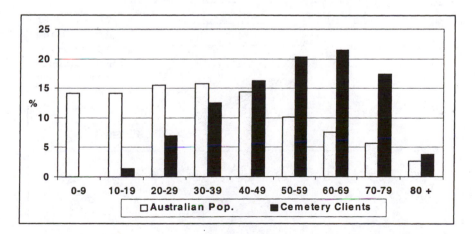

Figure 6.4 Ages of cemetery visitors compared with the general population.
Source: Bachelor [4].

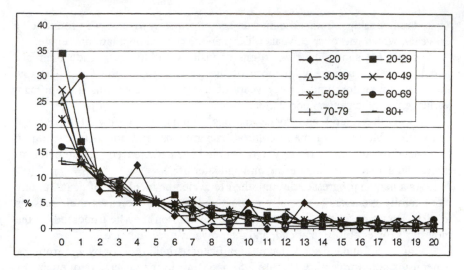

Figure 6.5 Proportions of visitors each year since death by age of the visitor.
Source: Bachelor [4].

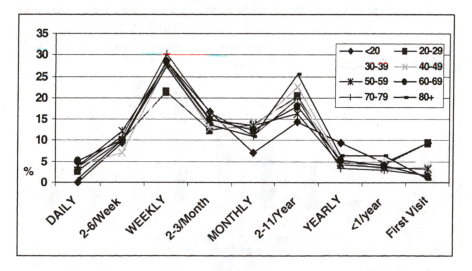

Figure 6.6 Proportions of visits at specific frequencies by age of the visitor.
Source: Bachelor [4].

Table 6.1. Median Age of Visitors
by
Relationship to the Deceased

Relationship of the Decedent	Median age of visitors
Grandparent	35
Parent	51
Brother/sister	53
Son/daughter	58
Spouse	68

Source: Bachelor [4].

management issues. Many visitors may have impaired vision and/or be less agile on their feet, to the extent that access may be more difficult for many cemetery visitors than for average members of the general population, particularly in low-maintenance cemeteries. Other issues relating to an older clientele include satisfactory public transport, and the provision and location of adequate toilets, shelters, and seating.

Raphael well describes her changing view of death through the life process:

> Man sets the thought of his own death aside in the years of his young adult life. He makes his family and embarks upon his achievements. Yet death will not be denied: in his middle years he glimpses it again, reminding him that his time is not infinite. In the latter half of his life, its reminders become more constant, more persistent. And, at last he meets it, fearfully or as a friend, his own, his personal death [1, p. 4].

Age is also a significant factor in common grief reactions. Sanders found that younger widows initially showed greater intensities of grief than older widows. However, when reviewed eighteen months later, she reports that the younger group generally displayed lower intensities. On the other hand, older spouses initially showed a diminished grief response, but this was often elevated by the later review. She suggests that the reactions of the different age groups relate to the younger group having adequate support and greater feelings of hope. Loneliness and anxiety were the greatest problems among the older group, with a sense of helplessness often expressed [2].

SEX

Bereavement researchers find several significant differences between the sexes in their typical responses to death [1, 2, 8-10, 12]. While some differences appear to be based on social conditioning, including traditional cultural roles, other behavioral variations evidently stem from intrinsic developmental differences. The sexes do not just differ biologically, but also psychologically and socially; and the differences between the sexes in their typical life spans may be attributed to a combination of biological, psychological, and social factors.

In relation to bereavement and cemetery visitation, behavioral differences between the sexes are linked to religiosity and the psychological personality trait of tender-mindedness. Francis [13] finds considerable evidence in Western Christian culture that girls and women display more signs of religiosity than boys and men, and separate research by both Ata [12] and Davies [14] support this contention. According to Francis, "females are more likely to believe in God, to attend public worship and to engage in personal prayer" [13], and Australian data also reveals a noticeably higher rate of religious commitment among females [15].

There is a clear inverse relationship between religiosity and the more masculine psychological personality dimension of psychoticism, according to Francis. And those who score high on psychoticism are found to condition less easily into tender-minded social attitudes, including religion [13].

Religion is a major factor in much cemetery visitation and, even among those of no religion, tender-mindedness is still a more feminine personality dimension, regardless of whether this is genetically determined or socially conditioned. It is therefore to be expected that cemetery visitation would be a more highly feminine activity.

The Visitation Study confirmed that many more females than males do visit cemeteries, as shown in Figure 6.7. While the general population is almost 50% male, cemetery visitors were found to be just over 64% female and just fewer than 36% male. As previously discussed, typical visits by females are also of significantly greater duration than are those of males (Figure 5.3, p. 53 [4]).

Factors relating to the number of female visitors include their concentration among the higher age brackets, as more women outlive their partners, and the higher incidence of visits among older people. But even more significant is the highly evident greater devotion among women to attending the graves or memorials of significant decedents.

No significant variation is evident between the sexes from the general pattern of decline in visitation over years since death, as shown in Figure 6.8. Similarly, no significant variation appears in the frequency of visits, as shown in Figure 6.9.

To enable direct comparison between the specific frequencies for each sex, proportions expressed in Figures 6.8 and 6.9 are of the respective sex, rather than of total visitors.

In contemporary Western societies, the average female outlives her male counterpart by around six years. However, when a further three years difference in the mean age at marriage is added to the average difference in lifespan, then a typical married woman may expect to be widowed for approximately nine years, and visit her husband's grave or memorial over much of this period.

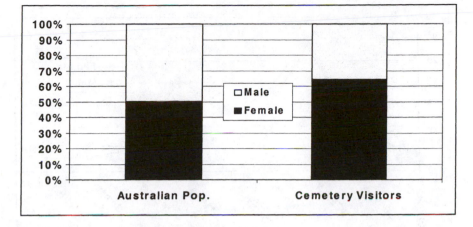

Figure 6.7 Sex of the general population and cemetery visitors.
Source: Bachelor [4].

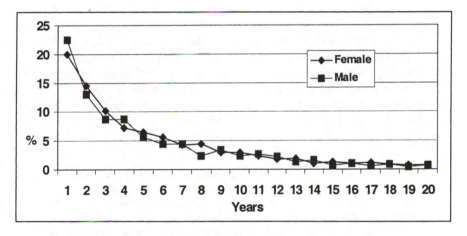

Figure 6.8 Proportions of visitors each year since death by sex of the visitor.
Source: Bachelor [4].

The similarity of a high proportion of weekly visits by both sexes is indicative of couples or families making regular religious pilgrimages to the cemetery in association with church attendance. This is particularly evident in cemetery compartments frequented by Italian Catholic and Greek Orthodox families. And the similarity of a high proportion of visits just a few times per year (2-11/year) is indicative of couples visiting graves or memorials on the most popular anniversaries.

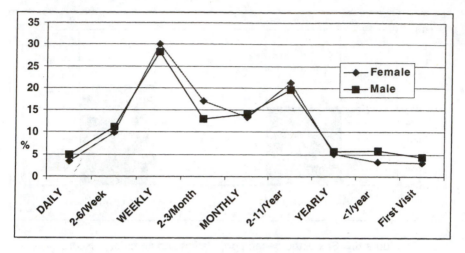

Figure 6.9 Proportions of visits at specific frequencies by sex of the visitor.
Source: Bachelor [4].

Across diverse sociocultural backgrounds, a person's sex is evidently a significant determinant of whether or not they will visit the cemetery, and if so, for how long. However, between the sexes there is no identifiable significant difference in either frequency or the general visitation trajectory.

Cemetery visitation is not the only bereavement behavior to differ between the sexes. Sanders identifies significant differences between the sexes in the typical coping methods employed:

> Because men depend on their wives for emotional support and nurturance, as well as an entrée to social interaction, when these services are no longer available, widowers have little practice or inclination to develop these new skills, but instead bury themselves in work. Women, on the other hand, cope by searching for social support, which in turn facilitates the bereavement process [2, p. 138].

Ata also found significant differences between the sexes on such matters as health problems, grief expressions, psychosomatic manifestations, and beliefs in an afterlife. According to Ata, the volume of emotional investment and depth of relationships is known to be more characteristic for females than males. He suggests that women tend to view an intimate relationship to be more important for their mental health and morale than occupational or social status [12].

Other studies have concluded that females are more likely than males to suffer post-bereavement psychological illness [1-3, 16], use chemical antidepressants [3], be religious [12, 13, 15], and be tender-minded [3, 13].

At the same time, bereaved males are reported to be more likely than females to display long-term signs of social withdrawal and disengagement [2], remarry sooner following the death of a spouse [8], and die of a heart attack after the loss of a spouse [3]. Different gender-related grief reactions may even be observed prior to adulthood, according to Parkes, who notes that boys more commonly express their grief in aggressive ways, while girls may become compulsive care-givers [3].

EDUCATION AND EMPLOYMENT

To date, no attempt has been made to identify any relationship between socioeconomic status and frequency of cemetery visitation. Socioeconomic status is a highly subjective concept, generally relating to factors such as education level, social and professional status, financial income, and accumulated wealth.

Within the Bereavement Study, education level and professional status were identified as partial indicators of socioeconomic status, though no data was gathered on subjects' financial income or accumulated wealth.

Among the 27 informants, purposively sampled primarily by religion and relationship to the deceased, 10 had undertaken some form of post-secondary education, ranging from technical certificate to doctoral degree. Table 6.2 shows the numbers and proportions (in parenthesis) of the samples of informants of higher and lower education levels visiting at various frequencies.

Within this albeit-small sample, the most frequent visitation (i.e., at least once per week and daily) was reported only among those less educated (47% of this group), while occasional visits and non-visitation were reported significantly more among the higher-educated informants (90% of this group). The limited data available therefore seems to suggest a strong negative correlation between level of education and frequency of cemetery visitation.

Table 6.2 Visitation Frequencies by Education Level

	Never	Occasional	At least 1/month	At least 1/week	Daily	Totals
No post-secondary education	1 (6%)	5 (29%)	3 (18%)	6 (35%)	2 (12%)	17 (100%)
Post-secondary education	3 (30%)	6 (60%)	1 (10%)	0 (0%)	0 (0%)	10 (100%)

Source: Bachelor [4].

Of the same 27 informants, nine could be classed as long-term unemployed, 12 as currently or recently sub-professionally employed, and six as currently or recently para-professionally or professionally employed. Table 6.3 shows the numbers and proportions (in parenthesis) of the samples of informants by employment status visiting at various frequencies.

A greater proportion of frequent visitation (i.e., at least once per week and daily) was reported among the long-term unemployed (44% of this group), slightly less among the sub-professional informants (35% of this group), and not at all among the professionals. Occasional visits and non-visitation were reported significantly more among the professional informants (83% of this group), and much less in both other groups (44% and 42%). Again, the limited data available appears to suggest a strong negative correlation between professionalism and frequency of cemetery visitation.

Further investigation, involving larger samples and the variables of income and wealth, may be required to determine precisely what factors are operating here. However, it appears that available time and employment status may be linked. Less positive outlook and social reinforcement, and chronic melancholia, may relate more to the unemployed and sub-professional mourners than to those of professional employment status.

However, it appears that there may well be a significant relationship between the average mourner's socioeconomic status and the typical frequency of their cemetery visitation.

CONCLUSION

This concludes our review of the main social determinants of cemetery visitation. The next chapter will identify the major cultural determinants of visitation.

Table 6.3 Visitation Frequencies by Professional Status

	Never	Occasional	At least 1/month	At least 1/week	Daily	Totals
Long-term unemployed	2 (22%)	2 (22%)	1 (11%)	3 (33%)	1 (11%)	9 (100%)
Sub-professional	0 (0%)	5 (42%)	3 (23%)	3 (23%)	1 (12%)	12 (100%)
Para-pro. & professional	2 (33%)	3 (50%)	1 (17%)	0 (0%)	0 (0%)	6 (100%)

Source: Bachelor [4].

REFERENCES

1. B. Raphael, *The anatomy of bereavement: A handbook for the caring professions*, Routledge, London, 1984.
2. C. M. Sanders, *Grief: The mourning after, dealing with adult bereavement*, Wiley Interscience, New York, 1989.
3. C. M. Parkes, *Bereavement: Studies of grief in adult life* (3rd ed.), Penguin, London, 1996.
4. P. Bachelor, *Cemetery visitation: The place of the cemetery in the grief process*, unpublished Ph.D. thesis, Charles Sturt University, Wagga Wagga, 2001.
5. G. Wretmark, A study in grief reaction, *Acta Psychiatrica et Neurologica Scandinavica Supplement, 136*, p. 29, 1959.
6. G. D. Gorer, *Death, grief and mourning*, Doubleday, New York, 1965.
7. E. A. Grollman (ed.), *Concerning death: A practical guide for the living*, Beacon Press, Boston, 1974.
8. M. Osterweis, F. Solomon, and M. Green (eds.), *Bereavement: Reactions, consequences, and care*, National Academy Press, Washington, D.C., 1984.
9. M. S. Stroebe, W. Stroebe, and R. O. Hansson (eds.), *Handbook of bereavement: Theory, research, and intervention*, Cambridge University Press, Cambridge, 1993.
10. T. A. Rando, *Treatment of complicated mourning*, Research Press, Champaign, Illinois, 1993.
11. Australian Bureau of Statistics, *Census of population and housing: Selected social and housing characteristics Australia,* Cat. No. 2015.0, ABS Canberra, 1997.
12. A. W. Ata, *Bereavement & health in Australia: Gender, psychological, religious and cross-cultural issues*, David Lovell, Melbourne, 1994.
13. L. J. Francis, Psychology of religion, in *The Penguin dictionary of religions*, J. R. Hinnells (ed.), Penguin, London, 1997.
14. D. J. Davies, *British attitudes towards reusing old graves,* Conference papers & reports, Proceedings of the Australian Cemeteries & Crematoria Association and International Cremation Federation, International Conference, Adelaide, October 13-17, 1996.
15. Australian Bureau of Statistics, *Classification counts: Religion,* Cat. No. 2022.0, ABS Canberra, 1997.
16. J. W. Worden, *Grief counselling and grief therapy: A handbook for the mental health practitioner* (2nd ed.), Routledge, London, 1991.

CHAPTER 7
Cultural Factors

In this chapter, we review cultural determinants of cemetery visitation, including religion of the family, nationality by which the family identifies itself, and choice of primary service (i.e., burial or cremation). It will become evident that practical bereavement behavior, including the visiting of graves and memorials, is significantly influenced by one's ethnicity.

The concept of ethnicity refers to a specific cultural group, within which one associates, and includes the demographic variables of nationality and religion.

Ethnicity is a significant determinant of primary service choice, memorial type, and frequency of cemetery visitation. *Primary service* refers to the initial service provided by a cemetery, crematorium, or memorial park, involving a choice between burial and cremation for the disposition of bodily remains.

Those who opt for cremation are much less likely to visit a cemetery than are those who choose burial and subsequently erect an elaborate monument. Those who do visit a cremation memorial typically attend much less frequently and for a shorter duration than do those visiting a grave.

RELIGION

Highly significant differences in attitudes to death, funeral rituals, and mourning responses occur between people of various faiths.

Figure 7.1 shows the proportions of cemetery visitors of major religions, within the Visitation Study, contrasted with the stated religions of the general population [1].

The major religious categories of Australian cemetery visitors were found to be Roman Catholic (comprising almost 27% of the population, but 44% of all cemetery visitors), Anglicans (23% of the population, and 18% of cemetery visitors), Orthodox (only 3% of the population, but 13% of cemetery visitors), and those with no religious affiliation (over 25% of the population, and just on 12% of cemetery visitors).

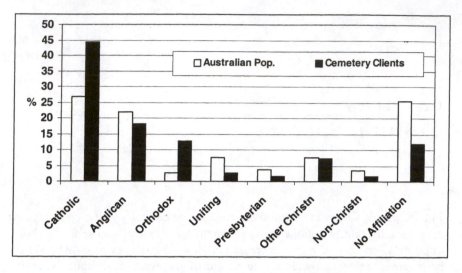

Figure 7.1 Major religions of Australian visitors contrasted with the general population. **Source:** Bachelor [2].

Although many may be only nominally affiliated with a religion indicated in a census, the association between funerals and religious services is still very strong. The proportionately low incidence of visitors of no religious affiliation also relates to the strong association between cemetery visitation and religious observance among some groups.

No significant variation from the general visitation trajectory (Figure 5.5, p. 55 [2]), by major religion, is evident in Figure 7.2. However, significant variation by religion is clearly apparent in the frequency of visits, as shown in Figure 7.3. It appears that religion has little, if any, effect on the normal course of grief, but clearly has a significant effect on cultural practices.

To enable direct comparisons between the specific frequencies for each religion, proportions expressed in Figures 7.2 and 7.3 are of the respective religions, rather than of total visitors.

Religion is evidently a significant determinant of more regular visits, as some 66% of Orthodox respondents reported that they visit *at least* once each week (i.e., Daily–Weekly), as did 49% of Catholics, but only 26% of Anglicans, and 27% of non-religiously-affiliated visitors. The data generally revealed close similarities between the frequencies of visits by Anglicans, other Protestant Christians, and the non-religiously-affiliated visitors.

A higher degree of religiosity is evident among families of non-Western European origin. Where funeral services were not conducted in accord with the rites of any particular faith, 86% of subsequent visitors identified the nationality of the deceased's family as that of a Western country.

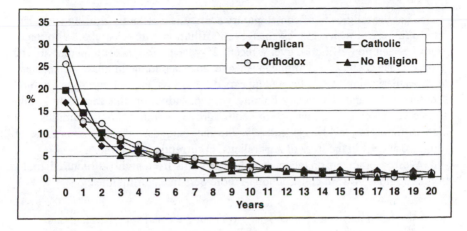

Figure 7.2 Proportions of visitors each year since death by selected religions. **Source:** Bachelor [2].

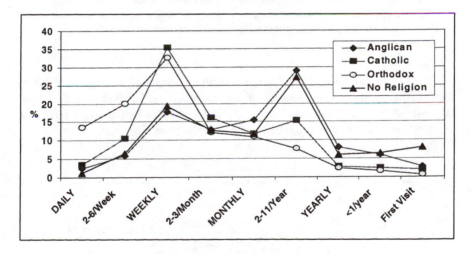

Figure 7.3 Proportions of visits at specific frequencies by selected religions. **Source:** Bachelor [2].

The religious mix of cemetery visitors was found to vary from the general population due to the greater frequencies of visits among specific ethnic groups, particularly Italian-Catholic, and Greek-Orthodox families.

The prevalence of Christians, and in particular Roman Catholics, relates to extra visits in association with Christmas and Easter periods, All Saints and All Souls Days. Orthodox Christmas and Easter and Hellenic name days are also very busy days in some cemeteries.

That the religiosity of contemporary society is constantly shifting is evident from Figure 7.4, which graphs changes in affiliation with Australia's two major churches and non-affiliates, over a recent 25-year period. Most apparent are the proportional decrease in Anglicanism and corresponding increase in apostasy and secularization. Catholicism appears to be less eroded by apostasy and secularization, and is virtually holding ground. However, this relatively steady state owes much to a higher rate of natural growth within Catholic families, and also to immigration [3]. Collectively, the data suggest that the importance of religion, at least in the lives of Australians, is currently in decline.

Walter comments on recent sociological shifts from highly-structured, traditional religions, toward construction of more personal spiritualities:

> If religion puts you in touch with a God out there and with meanings and mores external to the self, spirituality puts you in touch with your inner self and with the god within. Whereas the Catholic belongs to the one universal church and the Protestant chooses the church that seems right in the light of individual conscience, the new age believer takes individualism to its ultimate conclusion—listening to an inner voice to select bits and pieces from the gamut of world religions and folklore to create a personal spirituality [5, p. 28].

It is popularly understood that the sharing of common values and beliefs is important toward uniting members of human societies. Sanders considers that in the tragedy of a death, human social interaction is often given a religious interpretation, which she believes can be an important sustaining factor to the bereaved [6].

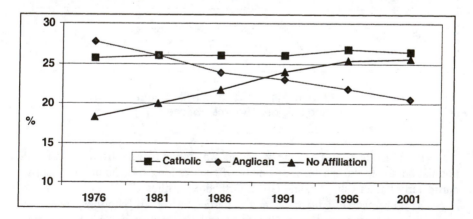

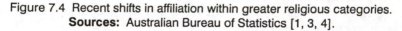

Figure 7.4 Recent shifts in affiliation within greater religious categories.
Sources: Australian Bureau of Statistics [1, 3, 4].

In seeking answers to new confronting issues, which may be beyond general human understanding, some metaphysical explanation is often sought to place a personal bereavement into a universal context [6]. Belief in an afterlife, as the basic tenet of most religions, also offers the bereaved an opportunity to mitigate their personal anxiety of final separation.

Parkes goes on to suggest that attempts to make sense of what has happened would seem to be one way of restoring what is lost by fitting its absence into some super-ordinate pattern [7]. Walter, in citing Malinowski [8], also considers that death, which he suggests of all human events is the most upsetting and disorganizing to man's calculation, is perhaps the main source of religious belief [5, 8].

The psychological and emotional ties of an intimate relationship are not easily severed by physical separation, but are, according to Ata, often strong enough to sustain the relationship and confirm for the bereaved the reality of life thereafter. And attempting to talk to the bereaved was also found to be quite common by Ata, who concludes that opting for comfort by illusions of the presence of the deceased is preferable to facing an unbearable reality of the finality of death [9]. However, it is suggested that these two positions are not necessarily mutually exclusive.

Religions are considered to play an important role in providing a set of satisfactory answers to many people [7, 9, 10]. Though as Raphael cautions, in each case the meaning and value of religious faith must be individually considered [10].

A strong relationship is apparent between religion and death anxiety. Researchers find that religious faith can give inner hope and a supportive social group to help the bereaved through their grief, or it can drive them to guilt and despair [7, 9, 10]. On one hand, religion is seen to function as a unifying force for many of the disruptive events which otherwise interfere with the continuity of routine life. On the other hand, many religions heighten anxieties with frightening images of judgment and damnation and by placing considerable demands on people in order for them to redeem their souls after death [7].

Christianity, Judaism, and Islam teach concepts of an afterlife spent in either heaven or hell. Heaven usually represents eternal bliss, while hell represents eternal torment. So, those who accept these teachings, but are not fully confident of either their own or the deceased's salvation, may thereby experience greater degrees of death-anxiety [7, 9, 10].

Several researchers have reported a curvilinear relationship between death anxiety and religiosity [7, 9, 10]. That is, those who are most committed (i.e., the very religious) and those most uncommitted (i.e., true atheists) both experience the least amount of fear, while those who fall in between (i.e., moderately committed believers) experience higher degrees of death anxiety. It is suggested by both Sanders and Ata that the moderately committed acquire the anxiety producing effects of religions without benefitting from the consolations which are only available through a high level of commitment and confidence [7, 9].

According to Parkes, the common view of God as a protecting, loving father is hard to maintain in the face of untimely bereavement, and the possibility of reunion in days to come does not help the widow tolerate the absence of her husband now. He also notes that faith in God and regular church attendance are not necessarily related to good outcomes following bereavement [8].

While at the time of a death, or occasion of a funeral, many people will re-identify with a familiar religious institution, personally held beliefs may not necessarily align with specific church doctrines. As Dyson suggests, the meanings of religion are quite problematic, as distinction between functional definitions (what a religion does) and substantive definitions (what a religion is) leaves many puzzles unresolved [11]. And Ata concludes that within many ethnic communities one's religion is determined largely by ancestry and not by personal conviction [9].

Religious affiliation also varies somewhat by sex. Although not necessarily reflecting any degree of religious commitment, Table 7.1 shows proportions of each sex identifying with selected major religions in Australia. Most major religions (and particularly the Uniting and Anglican churches) have a higher female following [4]. However, the Eastern Orthodox Church, Islam, and Hinduism appear exceptional in having more males than female adherents in Australia.

The greatest variations by sex, identified in Table 7.1, are among those affiliated with the Uniting Church, where there is an 8% variation in favor of

Table 7.1 Proportions of Each Sex
Identifying with Selected Major Religions

Religion	% Male	% Female
Uniting	45.8	54.2
Anglican	47.8	52.2
Judaism	48.3	51.7
Presbyterian	48.5	51.5
Catholic	48.6	51.4
Buddhism	48.6	51.4
Orthodox	51.1	48.9
Hinduism	51.9	48.1
Islam	52.4	47.6
No affiliation	53.5	46.5

Source: Australian Bureau of Statistics [4].

the more strongly represented females, and also among those of no religious affiliation, where a 7% variation occurs in favor of males.

It is clearly evident that many more people identify themselves as religious affiliates than actually practice any particular faith. While around 74% of the Australian population claim affiliation with a specific religion, Ata found less than 44% of respondents in his survey of bereaved families to attend a religious service at least once a month [9].

Affiliation with a religion does not necessarily mean that one upholds a belief in all of the basic tenets of that religion. Ata found that less than 73% of Australian-born Christians sampled believe that a soul goes to heaven or hell. And although he suggests it may be expected that Italian Catholics would believe a soul goes to heaven or hell, less than 36% of them in his study did believe so [9].

Beliefs in heaven and hell were also found by Ata to vary by gender, education level and age. Females, those less educated, and young to middle-aged people reported higher incidences of belief in a soul going to heaven or hell than did males, those with higher education, and of greater maturity [9].

In a British study, Davies found no more than 18% of those claiming adherence to the Catholic faith to believe in a resurrection, and only 4% of Anglicans to hold a similar confidence [12]. Sanders [6] refers to previous studies, by Gorer [13] and Marris [14], both of whom also found surprisingly low incidences of faith in an afterlife.

Some studies have found that twice as many women as men hold beliefs in an afterlife [7, 12]. Sanders also found that the death of a husband made widows even less confident in the possibility of immortality [6].

Parkes reminds us that the term quarantine comes from *quarantina*, the Italian for 40, which was the number of days of sequestration expected of the widow. He suggests that an accepted mourning period provides social sanction for beginning and ending grief, and is clearly likely to have psychological value for the bereaved. Recognizing variation among individual needs, Parkes adds that the absence of any social expectations, as is common in Western cultures today, leaves bereaved people confused and insecure in their grief. He further suggests that a clear lead from the churches in this matter would be psychologically helpful to many bereaved people [7].

SPECIFIC RELIGIOUS PRACTICES

Religion is well identified as a significant variable in grieving [7, 15-19].

Judaism is highly prescriptive of certain periods within which specific activities and mourning rituals are to be observed. It offers fascinating, complex, traditional mourning rituals which, although highly-legalistic and temporally-dogmatic, appear to channel bereaved Jews through stages similar to those proposed by some contemporary psychologists.

There is a 30-day period of ritualistic mourning, except for when the deceased is a parent of the bereaved, then the complete mourning period is a full year [15, 20]. Mourning is to be strictly limited to the given periods and customary observances, as excessive grief may be taken as want of trust in God [15].

Jews are required to observe three specific stages of mourning: aninut, shivah, and sheloshim [20].

Aninut is the period between death and burial, which should be within 24 hours according to Jewish law. Garments are rent on word of the death. In recognition of the mourners troubled mind during this time of most despair, social amenities and also religious requirements are canceled. No personal grooming, including shaving, is carried out.

Shivah is the seven days following burial, during which the bereaved remain within the home. For the first three days of shivah, visiting is discouraged and the mourner doesn't respond to greetings. After the first three days of shivah the "inner freezing" begins to thaw as the mourner emerges from intense grief, talks about their loss, and accepts consolation from others.

Sheloshim is the 30 days following burial (including shivah). After shivah, the mourner is encouraged to leave the house and commence rejoining society. Rent clothing is still worn for deceased parents, and males still don't shave or cut their hair until the end of sheloshim.

In Jewish tradition, if an infant does not live for at least 30 days they are not considered "viable." According to Lamm, other than the last purification rites and a simple burial with three persons present, traditional mourning and funeral rites are not observed [20]. However, some Jewish burial societies do now concede that a modern Jewish mother may be permitted, and possibly should even be encouraged, to mourn a perinatal loss.

In accord with ancient custom, Jews should seek to purchase a grave and own it outright before they die. The grave must be in a specific Jewish cemetery, or at least within a Jewish section of a general cemetery with separate entrance and facilities for Jews and non-Jews. Burial must also be permanent, as it is offensive and defiling to disinter a decayed corpse [20].

To Jews, the holiness of the cemetery is equivalent to the holiness of the sanctuary, and there are stipulations on who may be buried next to whom. Appropriate cemetery visitation is to be observed by Jews. Cemetery etiquette also requires one to dress properly for the occasion, and one must not step over a grave or sit on a monument. Eating, drinking, and any other frivolous or pleasurable activities desecrates the cemetery and violates codes of honor [20].

Visitation should not be excessive, nor should it be neglected. Graves are to be visited at proper times including days of calamity or decisive moments in life, but not on holy days. Proper times include the concluding days of the mourning periods shivah and sheloshim, fast days, and the memorial anniversary (*yahrzeit*). A commemorative monument unveiling and dedication service occurs at the cemetery between the end of shivah and yahrzeit [20].

Other religions employ different rituals in seeking to help their constituents through long-term mourning and acceptance of their losses within teachings of the faith.

Islam requires a Muslim to be buried as soon as possible after a death. This is to be on the same day if at all practical, as the Prophet himself recommends immediate burial [21].

Males ceremoniously wash and dress male bodies: females do so for deceased females. Great discretion is required of those involved. The body is dressed in three layers of cotton shroud from top to bottom.

A funeral service is held at the mosque prior to burial in a cemetery. Traditionally, the body is buried without a coffin to be in contact with the soil to which it must return. Natural decomposition is not to be delayed.

Orientation of the grave depends on its geographic location and placement of the corpse must be such that the decedent faces Mecca. The body is placed in the grave by either Islamic funeral service staff or family members.

Traditionally, stones are placed around the corpse and a cover of timber boards is then laid prior to backfilling the grave. As a mark of respect, all the men usually help with backfilling, though cemetery employees may complete this task.

Women do not customarily approach the grave, as they are considered more emotional than men, and it is not to the deceased's benefit to have them crying loudly over the body. Even though the soul has left the body, it can still sense what is going on around the body.

After the funeral, mourners often return to the home of the decedent. Family and friends stay with a grieving spouse for at least three days. Islam holds a prescribed mourning period of three days, during which the bereaved stay home and are condoled by visitors, and then all are required to resume normal activities.

A traditional grave is a simple mound with a low marker, and possibly some greenery. Islam does not prescribe or recommend specific cemetery visitation. It is up to the individual to visit as frequently as desired.

A Muslim should remarry soon after the death of a spouse, as there are to be no hermits in Islam. However, a woman may not remarry within four months and ten days, so that any recent conception may be identified as the child of her late husband. But a man may remarry as soon as he desires [21].

Hinduism is not dogmatic on what happens to the soul after death. Life does not end, but the soul passes on to another form depending on the degree of good or bad karma one has attained. While some Hindus may seek reincarnation, in either human, animal or god form, others seek to be freed from the cycle of rebirth [22, 23]. Hindus are discouraged from displaying emotions, and, according to Ata, depression arises from ignorance or denial of Hindu knowledge [9]. Traditionally, Hindus are cremated following an elaborate ritual involving offerings to ancestors and participating priests.

Buddhism holds the basic laws of karma and the goal of liberation (*moksha*) from the round of rebirth (*samsara*) in common with Hinduism [22]. It is suggested by Ata that Buddhists, understanding the transience of death, tend to accept the mourning process serenely [9]. Buddhist funereal practices vary somewhat between different countries and different forms of Buddhism. While within some traditions Buddhists must be cremated, others prefer to bury their deceased.

The **Roman Catholic** Church provides for Month's Mind Mass being observed one month after the death and funeral liturgy, and an Anniversary Mass being celebrated each year after the funeral liturgy [24]. However, for practical reasons, many Catholic Churches no longer specifically provide for an Anniversary Mass, finding parishioners are usually satisfied with specific mention of a decedent's name during a normal mass around the anniversary of their death. Catholics are more commonly buried than cremated, and although it is now acceptable to the Church, cremation was officially condemned for much of last century.

Eastern Orthodox Churches observe ritual blessings of the grave at various intervals, including the day after the funeral, nine-days later, six-weeks, three-months, nine-months, and twelve-months after the funeral liturgy. Some families thereafter maintain annual memorial services for many years. Cremation is generally not acceptable within the Orthodox faith.

Protestant Christian rituals vary among the diverse divisions of the faith, and this is compounded by a degree of self-interpretation allowed within most Protestants churches. Typically, a funeral involves certain religious observances, but the deceased may be either buried or cremated, and there are no prescribed subsequent memorial services.

Chinese immigrants comprise a particular cultural group for whom Western cemeteries may need to make special dispensations.

Feng shui, the ancient Chinese theory of design and placement is applied by many Chinese people to burial and memorialization. Modern feng shui is derived from ancient classics, including the Book of Burial written in the fourth century B.C. [25].

The aim of feng shui, literally meaning the flow of wind and water, is to enhance well-being through maintaining harmony and balance between the energy flows of humans, earth and heaven [26, 27]. People are affected, either positively or negatively, by their surroundings, with some places being notice-ably luckier, happier, healthier or more peaceful than others [27].

Fundamental to good feng shui is a balance between yin (passive, feminine) and yang (active, masculine) qualities, within the constantly changing elements or forces of nature.

An ideal site for a house (or a grave, being the home of the dead) is usually halfway up a hill where the descending heaven life-force meets the ascending earth life-force. The site will be shouldered by hills on either side, and with water, not likely to flood the site, in front [26, 27]. Some believe that the remains of male ancestors are conduits of a force that influences the fortunes of descendants, and that a grave well sited where the cosmic breath is powerfully focused will enhance the material fortunes of living descendants.

The orientation of a grave is a crucial feng shui consideration, as is the day and time of interment. While some people hire the services of a feng shui master for such important decisions, it is cheaper to buy an almanac which offers useful advice on grave alignment, as well as auspicious dates for funerals, marriages and so on [25].

But simply siting a grave well is not enough in itself. The Chinese tradition of ancestor worship requires regular visits to the grave, including offerings to the deceased to ensure their comfort in the spirit world, and seeking their continued blessings and good fortune for survivors.

The site of the entire cemetery, in relation to residential housing and local businesses, will be of significance to many Chinese, as overlooking or being overlooked by a cemetery are believed to bring bad fortune [25].

NATIONALITY

The national identity of a family is a significant factor in influencing the visitation activities of its members.

As national identification can be a complex concept, personal perception of the nationality by which members of the decedent's family most identify themselves was chosen to indicate national identity, rather than any imposed classification, such as country of birth. Consequently, in many instances, the attribute *Australian* may represent an adopted nationality, and does not necessarily indicate the country of birth of either the decedent or the visitor.

Just less than half of all participants in the Visitation Study identified their family as Australian. Figure 7.5 shows that following Australian, the major nationalities of cemetery visitors include Italian, Greek, British, Maltese, Polish, and Croatian. The category *Other* included virtually all other nationalities represented throughout Australia, but with each identifiable group comprising no more than 1% of all cemetery visitors.

No significant variation from the general visitation trajectory (Figure 5.5, p. 55) by major nationality is evident in Figure 7.6. However, significant variation by nationality is clearly apparent in the frequency of visits, as shown in Figure 7.7. To enable direct comparisons between the specific frequencies for each nationality, proportions expressed in Figures 7.6 and 7.7 are of the respective nationalities rather than of total visitors.

Nationality is evidently a significant determinant of visitation frequency, with 71% of Greek respondents reporting that they visit *at least* once each week (i.e., Daily–Weekly); while 58% of Italian, 31% of British, and only 27% of Australian visitors reported similar frequencies.

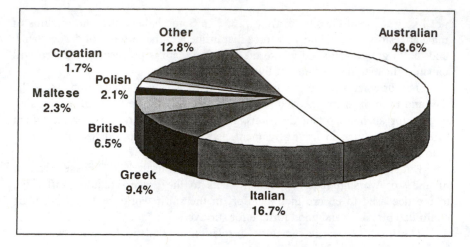

Figure 7.5 Nationality by which members of the family most
identify themselves. **Source:** Bachelor [2].

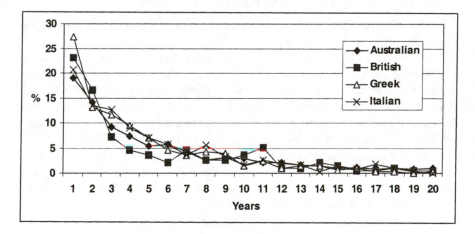

Figure 7.6 Proportions of visitors each year since death by
selected nationalities. **Source:** Bachelor [2].

The correlation between nationality and religion is very strong, with both variables comprising common concepts of ethnicity. Figure 7.8 reveals that of Italian visitors, virtually 98% identified their relevant family religion as Catholic, as did virtually 96% of Croatian and Maltese, and 92% of Polish visitors. Of Greeks, 98% identified their family religion as Orthodox. Australian and British visitors were predominantly of various Christian faiths, with the Anglican Church

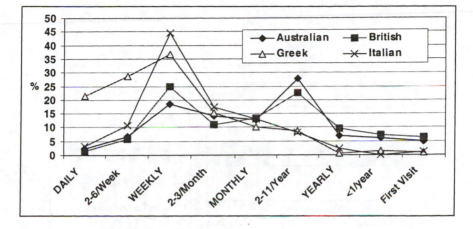

Figure 7.7 Proportions of visits at specific frequencies by selected nationalities. **Source:** Bachelor [2].

most popular among both nationalities. The data table attached to Figure 7.8 clarifies the specific proportions of each faith identified among visitors of specific nationalities.

Retention of religious identity is evidently very strong among Catholic and Orthodox immigrant families. Over 93% of both Greek-born and Italian-born residents identify their religions as Orthodox and Catholic respectively, and similarly, 74% of Irish-born residents as Catholic. The first generation of Australian-born adult-children to Greek, Italian and Irish immigrants each reveals a decrease of only 1% in their respective family's religious identity [28].

Concepts of multiculturalism and non-discrimination were embraced by many cemeteries during the 1980s, with the effect that compartmentalization by religion is not usually now practiced in new developments. However, while non-denominational, or multi-denominational, compartments may sound appealing to remotely concerned but uninvolved observers, this practice actually offends the traditions of many religious groups. It is clearly not what many cemetery stakeholders really want, and it also makes things extremely difficult, if not impossible, for cemetery managers to identify and meet the needs of their respective clients through specific cultural market segmentation.

Where variety is still offered in graves and monumental styles at larger general cemeteries, clustering by choice of various cultures is highly evident. And several religious groups, some of which have successfully lobbied for their own exclusive cemeteries, continue to express their preference for this form of discrimination.

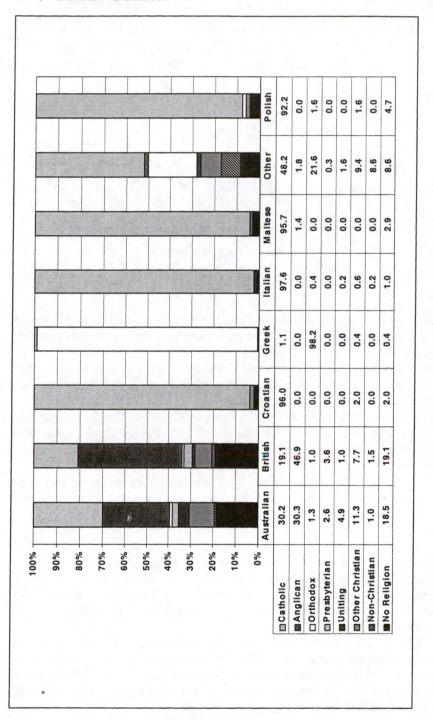

	Australian	British	Croatian	Greek	Italian	Maltese	Other	Polish
Catholic	30.2	19.1	96.0	1.1	97.6	95.7	48.2	92.2
Anglican	30.3	46.9	0.0	0.0	0.0	1.4	1.8	0.0
Orthodox	1.3	1.0	0.0	98.2	0.4	0.0	21.6	1.6
Presbyterian	2.6	3.6	0.0	0.0	0.0	0.0	0.3	0.0
Uniting	4.9	1.0	0.0	0.0	0.2	0.0	1.6	0.0
Other Christian	11.3	7.7	2.0	0.4	0.6	0.0	9.4	1.6
Non-Christian	1.0	1.5	0.0	0.0	0.2	0.0	8.6	0.0
No Religion	18.5	19.1	2.0	0.4	1.0	2.9	8.6	4.7

Figure 7.8 Faiths of visitors of major nationalities. **Source:** Bachelor [2].

Within Australia, around 46% of cemetery visitors are of families whose first language is other than English. An implication of this is the likelihood of significant numbers of visitors not being able to adequately understand informative and regulatory signs and other printed materials. In such a multicultural facility as a large general cemetery, international symbolism may be required.

Different emotional responses between modern Anglo-based and other European cultures in their typical grief expression, and also in memorialization behavior, are well noted [9, 10, 29]. Within some cultures, the open expression of grief is expected, and, as Raphael suggests, within Italian and Greek communities it would be considered shameful if tears were not shed and emotions freely displayed [10]. However, even among these groups, wailing is generally considered more acceptable among women [9]. Within Western cultures, restraint from showing distress is generally encouraged and strong emotional control is praised; and as Raphael observes, this release is often also denied to women [10].

The degree to which various cultures or societies expect and encourage a sharing of experiences about the dead person after a funeral varies enormously. The Irish wake, with its alcohol, shared emotions and experiences, provides a strong contrast to the solitary, somber Jewish shivah. But some forms of ritualistic mourning may not always be evident to the observer. Raphael further suggests that while the process may be clearly spelled out in some cultures by prescribed clothes and behaviors, such as the wearing of black and avoidance of social occasions, in other cultures the requirements may also be specific but covert [10].

Ata believes that particular compounding problems arise for migrants who hold dearly the values and practices of their ancestors and country of birth, but are now forced to conform to a large extent with the dictates of their host country. He reports noticeable conflicts between burial instructions, Western law and mourning practices, and various ethnic backgrounds causing frustration and compounding the grief of migrants [9].

Walter also identifies conflict between traditional and modern generations, within the same family, being present in many immigrant families. He suggests that the first generation needs to die and mourn according to the traditions of their religion, while their children want to do the right thing by their aging parents but don't know what the right thing is [5].

He further notes that:

> Americans tend to construct themselves in a more modern/postmodern way, while Europeans do so in a more traditional way. An English person, for example, knows who they are, identifying a place within a certain social class where one might almost say they belong. French, Swiss and Italians more clearly embrace gender stereotypes. The American, by contrast, believes every individual must create him or herself and so has to continuously create an identity [5, p. 53].

PRIMARY SERVICE

Emotional, spiritual, social, and other community values of cemeteries are often overlooked. However, their practical value in the disposition of human remains is generally well regarded as the primary reason for their existence. However, this represents only an *initial* or primary service provided to mourners. Such primary services include burial and cremation.

More than half of all Australian funerals currently involve cremation; yet, as Figure 7.9 shows, only one-fifth of all cemetery visits are made to cremation memorials. There are two main reasons for this. Firstly, many cremated remains are not interred within cemeteries. Secondly, those who maintain a stronger association with the body of their deceased are more inclined to choose burial and to visit more frequently. The latter tends to be the case with Southern European families, and among those of other ethnicities including Westerners who have lost a child. Although stillborn babies are just as likely to be cremated as buried, around ten times as many deceased children are buried than are cremated.

Other studies have also found mourners to retain a greater affinity with buried bodies than cremated remains. In his study of London widows, Parkes found that, on the whole, the sense of the dead person being located in his place of burial was less strong when he had been cremated, and that the reality of death seemed somehow more final following cremation than occurred following burial. Parkes also found that although some widows in his London

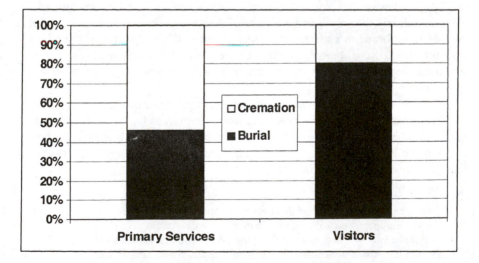

Figure 7.9 Proportions of burials and cremation services and their subsequent visits. **Source:** Bachelor [2].

study subsequently visited the crematorium, entered their husband's name in the Book of Remembrance, and attended memorial services, there were fewer tendencies to feel close to the dead person at the crematorium than at the cemetery. Several widows, he says, regarded this as a distinct disadvantage of cremation [5].

Cremation often results in no commemoration within a memorial park or cemetery. Some funeral directors encourage families to authorize them to collect cremated remains on the family's behalf, but often no decision on the ultimate destination of the remains is then made. Currently in Australia, around 51% of cremated remains are collected, 7% are scattered by request, and just 42% are interred within cemeteries, sometimes in existing family graves, but more commonly within specific memorial gardens.

Today in many modern cities, thousands of cremated remains lie hidden in garages and hall cupboards. Some sit proudly on mantle pieces, but often only one elderly family member knows where they are. Many more unclaimed remains languish in funeral home storage spaces. This does not help other grieving family members who may need a special place to visit at certain times. And whoever eventually clears out the house or funeral home may be unrelated and quite dispassionate about the ultimate fate of any unwanted item such as a box of ashes.

Figure 7.10 reveals no significant variation by type of service, within the visitation trajectory. This indicates a similar emotional response and wane in visitation regardless of primary service. However, significant variation in the frequency of visits is clearly apparent by type of service, as shown in Figure 7.11.

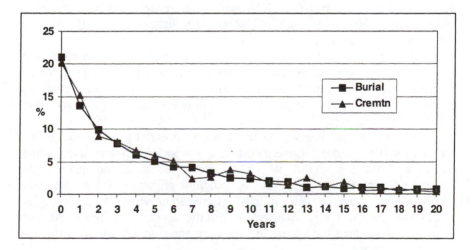

Figure 7.10 Proportions of visitors each year since death by primary service. **Source:** Bachelor [2].

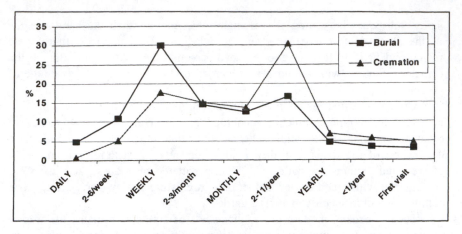

Figure 7.11 Proportions of visits at specific frequencies by primary service. **Source:** Bachelor [2].

To enable direct comparisons between the specific trends and frequencies for each type of service, burials and cremations are expressed in Figures 7.10 and 7.11 as proportions of the respective service type, rather than of total services.

Where the deceased were buried, over 45% of subsequent visits are made *at least* once a week (i.e., Daily–Weekly). But where the deceased were cremated, less than 24% of subsequent visits are made *at least* once a week. And those who cremate are much more likely to visit less frequently than once a month, but more than once a year (i.e., 2-11/year). This frequency includes common and personal anniversaries, such as Mothers Day, Fathers Day, birthdays, and the anniversary of death.

Funeral and memorialization practices are strongly tied to tradition, and cultural factors greatly influence subsequent visitor rates. The strong correlation between cultural background and choice of service is clearly evident from the proportions of burials and cremation services in selected countries, as shown in Table 7.2 [30].

Dominant religion is a significant factor, with burial usually required by people of Roman Catholic, Eastern Orthodox, Jewish and Islamic faiths, while cremation is the first choice of Hindus, some Buddhists, and increasingly Protestant Christians and those with no religious affiliation. Other important factors in determining the choice of burial or cremation include the practicalities of available land and fuel resources in specific countries of origin. Among migrant families, these traditional practices are commonly transmitted to subsequent generations.

Burials are evidently followed by several times the volume of cemetery visits than are cremation services. This relates primarily to the preference for

Table 7.2 Burial and Cremation Services
in Selected Countries

Country	% Burials	% Cremations
Australia	46	54
Canada	54	46
China	53	47
France	81	19
Germany	60	40
Great Britain	29	71
Greece	100	0
Ireland	95	5
Italy	94	6
Japan	1	99
United States	73	27

Source: International Cremation Federation [30].

burial among the most frequent-visiting cultural groups, and a preference for cremation by those less likely to visit frequently.

The proportion of commemorative visits varies considerably between cemeteries. The ethnic mix, including religions and nationalities, of a cemetery's client catchment is an evident external factor, but the primary service, or services, offered and the cemetery's memorial policies (i.e., what is provided and permitted) evidently influence the choice of a cemetery and the visitation patterns of specific groups.

The Visitation Study included a monumental cemetery (providing burial only) and a memorial park (including lawn cemetery, crematorium, and memorial gardens) within 15 minutes travel time of each other. Though the average number of annual visits to a cemetery per annual primary service was just under 250, the monumental cemetery had the particularly high visitation rate of over 600 per primary service, and the memorial park had the particularly low rate of less than 80.

While the two cemeteries in this example clearly have extensively overlapping client catchments, significant characteristic differences can be seen to account for extreme differences in the numbers of memorial visits. The monumental cemetery's primary services are all burials, while 70% of the memorial park's services are cremations. The particular memorial park does not permit use of any above ground monuments, such as predominate the cemetery and are commonly preferred by Italian and Greek families living in the locality.

Consequently, the cemetery's visitor nationality profile included 22% Italian and 16% Greek, while the memorial park's visitor profile was just 13% Italian and 1% Greek. And from almost six times as many primary services as the monumental cemetery, within one year the memorial park derived only twice the cemetery's income.

This example illustrates that, akin with many other businesses, where a cemetery does not provide the type of services sought by its market, its potential clients will seek out and find more appropriate services elsewhere.

Market research presented at a convention of the Cremation Association of North America concluded that perceived dignity and simplicity are the main reasons people opt for cremation. The convention also heard that people choose cremation for themselves mainly to place less of a burden on survivors, and for environmental reasons. Only one-third of people surveyed cited cost, placing it among other, lesser reasons for choosing cremation over burial [31].

CONCLUSION

This concludes the review of major cultural determinants of cemetery visitation, and also concludes Part B, which presented major findings of the quantitative Visitation Study of cemetery visitation. The following Part C presents key findings of the qualitative Bereavement Study.

REFERENCES

1. Australian Bureau of Statistics, *Census of population and housing: Selected social and housing characteristics Australia*, Cat. No. 2015.0, ABS, Canberra, 1997.
2. P. Bachelor, *Cemetery visitation: The place of the cemetery in the grief process*, unpublished Ph.D. thesis, Charles Sturt University, Wagga Wagga, 2001.
3. Australian Bureau of Statistics, *Year book Australia 1997*, Cat. No. 1301.0, A.G.P.S., Canberra, 1997.
4. Australian Bureau of Statistics, *Classification counts: Religion*, Cat. No. 2022.0, ABS, Canberra, 1997.
5. J. A. Walter, *The revival of death*, Routledge, London, 1994.
6. C. M. Sanders, *Grief: The mourning after, dealing with adult bereavement*, Wiley Interscience, New York, 1989.
7. C. M. Parkes, *Bereavement: Studies of grief in adult life* (3rd ed.), Penguin, London, 1996.
8. B. Malinowski, The role of magic and religion, in *Reader in comparative religion*, W. H. Lessa and E. Z. Vogt (eds.), Evanston, Row Peterson (1931), 1962.
9. A. W. Ata, *Bereavement & health in Australia: Gender, psychological, religious and cross-cultural issues*, David Lovell, Melbourne 1994.
10. B. Raphael, *The anatomy of bereavement: A handbook for the caring professions*, Routledge, London, 1984.
11. A. Dyson, Secularisation, in *The Penguin dictionary of religions*, J. R. Hinnells (ed.), Penguin, London, 1997.

12. D. J. Davies, *British attitudes towards reusing old graves,* Conference papers & reports, Proceedings of the Australian Cemeteries & Crematoria Association and International Cremation Federation, International Conference, Adelaide, October 13-17, 1996.

13. G. D. Gorer, *Death, grief and mourning,* Doubleday, New York, 1965.

14. P. Marris, *Widows and their families,* Routledge & Kegan Paul, London, 1968.

15. E. A. Grollman (ed.), *Concerning death: A practical guide for the living,* Beacon Press, Boston, 1974.

16. M. Osterweis, F. Solomon, and M. Green (eds.), *Bereavement: Reactions, consequences, and care,* National Academy Press, Washington, D.C., 1984.

17. N. O'Connor, *Letting go with love: The grieving process,* La Mariposa, Arizona, 1986.

18. M. S. Stroebe, W. Stroebe, and R. O. Hansson (eds.), *Handbook of bereavement: Theory, research, and intervention,* Cambridge University Press, Cambridge, 1993.

19. T. A. Rando, *Treatment of complicated mourning,* Research Press, Champaign, Illinois, 1993.

20. M. Lamm, *The Jewish way in death and mourning,* Jonathon David, New York, 1969.

21. Sheikh Fehmi Naji El Imam, personal communication, Omar Sheikh Khatab Mosque, Melbourne, May 11, 1998.

22. R. Gethin, Buddhism, in *The Penguin dictionary of religions,* J. R. Hinnells (ed.), Penguin, London, 1997.

23. Microsoft®, Encarta, 1994.

24. R. J. Butler, The Roman Catholic way in death and mourning, in *Concerning death: A practical guide for the living,* E. A. Grollman (ed.), Beacon Press, Boston, 1974.

25. E. Teather, *Planning for death in Hong Kong, The Australian city—Future/past,* Proceedings of the Third Australian Planning History Conference, Monash University, Melbourne, 1997.

26. S. McFarlane, Feng shui, in *The Penguin dictionary of religions,* J. R. Hinnells (ed.), Penguin, London, 1997.

27. B. Henwood and H. Choy, *Feng Shui,* Lansdowne, Sydney, 1997.

28. Australian Bureau of Statistics, *Australian social trends,* Cat. No. 4102.0, ABS, Canberra, 2002.

29. C. Sagazio, *Cemeteries: Our heritage,* National Trust of Australia (Victoria), Melbourne, 1992.

30. International Cremation Federation, International cremation statistics, *Pharos International, 68*(4), pp. 26-37, 2002.

31. American Cemetery, What do consumers want?, *American Cemetery, 68*(11), pp. 26-48, 1996.

Part C

In Part B, we reviewed major findings of the quantitative cemetery Visitation Study, identified the volume of cemetery visits, common visitation patterns, and general social and cultural significance of visitation.

Part C now presents key findings of the qualitative Bereavement Study, and identifies personal values of the cemetery to mourners within different social and cultural contexts. This part considers reasons for visitation and non-visitation, major activities and emotions of visitors, and what visitors feel about their frequency of visitation and its role in working through grief.

CHAPTER 8

Visitation Reasons

This chapter presents an account of self-reported common reasons why mourners actually visit cemeteries. The Bereavement Study revealed that there are three principal reasons and several less-significant reasons for visitation, as well as several reasons for not visiting [1]. The principle reasons for visiting are to fulfill a sense of obligation, to maintain a significant emotional bond, and to seek solace from the emotions of grief.

Of 27 informants in the Bereavement Study, four were non-visitors and 22 discussed their reasons for visiting and/or reasons for not visiting.

OBLIGATION

Two-thirds of those interviewed in the Bereavement Study referred either directly or indirectly to a sense of obligation toward visiting the grave or memorial of a loved one. Such a perceived obligation may be felt to the decedent, the family, or to the visitor him/herself; or it may relate to the expectations of others. Other reasons for visiting that relate to a sense of obligation include a religious duty, some perceived duty of respect, and an inexplicable innate compulsion to visit.

The following verbatim comments illustrate typical sentiments expressed toward fulfilling a sense of obligation or duty, respectively to the decedent, the family, and to one's self.

> I'll keep going; I promised my father I'd keep going for him.
>
> *47-year-old, Australian daughter of no specific faith,*
> *bereaved 5 months*

> At first after she died, every time I drove past, I used to feel that I had to go, otherwise I was somehow letting the side down.
>
> *62-year-old, Australian non-religious husband,*
> *bereaved 4½ years*

I think it is perhaps a sense of duty that I feel to go there now. I feel it's a duty to me, because—it's a silly thought—if you don't go, you feel that you're forgetting the person.

45-year-old, Australian non-religious female
secret-lover, bereaved 3 years

An obligation can also relate to fulfilling a perceived expectation of others, as expressed in the study by two non-religious husbands. One of these men expressed his feelings this way:

In the beginning, people expect you to go there. If I were really truthful, I'd probably have to say that most of the times I went were because people expected me to. To be honest, I felt a bit guilty if I hadn't been when people thought I should have. Now I go when I want to go: when I feel like it, and not when other people think I should be going.

51-year-old, Australian non-religious husband,
bereaved 2 months

Several other mourners spoke of their religious duty to visit, including two Italian Catholic widows who both considered that their faith plays a significant role in the frequently of their visits.

The Catholic thing to do is go once a week. It is a religious obligation and a duty to [my husband] and to God.

70-year-old, Italian Catholic wife, bereaved 3 years

Of course, that's what you feel. That's why you go into the cemetery, because if not that feeling, well what for do you go?

66-year-old, Italian Catholic wife, bereaved 5 years

However, a somewhat less-traditional younger man revealed that not all Italian Catholic mourners feel the same obligation:

I don't visit out of any religious obligation, purely out of a feeling that I should see Dad.

40-year-old, Italian Catholic son, bereaved 3 years

Although neither Roman Catholicism nor Islam specifically encourages or discourages cemetery visitation, to some bereaved adherents of both faiths, some perception of a religious obligation to visit evidently does exist.

A special day for Muslims on Fridays. . . . It is very important to be there, especially on Fridays. I come every Friday, and sometimes on Sundays or Saturdays.

52-year-old, Turkish Muslim father, bereaved 14 months

As discussed in the previous chapter, Judaism requires appropriate cemetery visitation to be observed, including avoidance of the extremes of constant visitation and neglect. Graves are to be visited at proper times, including days of significance, but not holy days. Accordingly, a Jewish informant in the Bereavement Study advised that:

> After a funeral, the immediate family is not permitted to go to the cemetery for thirty days or four weeks, so as a family, we all went four weeks later. After the thirty days, we have a special service. . . . Jewish law actually states that it is more important to go to the cemetery on important days like birthdays, memorial days, prior to high holidays and the anniversary of the death. It is not required to go daily, weekly or on a fortnightly basis and have a routine. Some people would actually condemn frequent visitation to the cemetery.
>
> *37-year-old, Australian Jewish sister,*
> *bereaved 8 months*

But no Protestant Christians in the study considered their cemetery visitation to be at all influenced by their faith.

A few mourners commented on a perceived duty of respect as a reason for visiting the cemetery.

> I sort of felt that somehow it would be disrespectful, selfish, in bad taste, not to go in there. . . . There's not a sense of visiting her, but there is a sense of duty done and respecting a memory: of ensuring that anybody else who goes there will see that the memory is respected and not neglected.
>
> *62-year-old, Australian non-religious husband,*
> *bereaved 4½ years*

Some people identified respect as a reason for paying secondary visits to other relatives, while they were in the cemetery primarily to visit a specific closer relative.

> I sometimes do the rounds of the family, but that's more out of respect than anything else, if I've got time. . . . I would've gone to visit my grandparents just purely through respect, but with my father, it's a bit more. There is more emotion attached to the visit, because it's my father.
>
> *40-year-old, Italian Catholic son, bereaved 3 years*

Compulsive visitation was identified among several mourners, most of whom were mothers.

> I have to come and see him; I have to look after him. . . . I have to do something. I can't do anything for him at home, so I have to come and just talk to him. People might think I'm being silly. But quite frankly, I don't care what people think. That's my child there, and this is the last thing I can do for him.
>
> *33-year-old, Australian Catholic mother,*
> *bereaved 2 years*

But the reports of some others reveal that this behavior is not just limited to mothers.

> I go every day, and it just helps me to sleep.
>
> *66-year-old, Maltese Catholic husband, bereaved 4½ years*

Within the study, compulsive visitation appeared more common shortly after the loss of a child or a spouse, but was also found to persist in cases of complicated mourning and chronic grief.

EMOTIONAL BOND

More than half of those in the Bereavement Study who visit a cemetery discussed issues pertaining to their maintenance of a significant emotional bond with the decedent. Talking to the decedent, maintaining the monument, and placing gifts were the most commonly expressed graveside activities undertaken by mourners toward maintaining emotional bonds.

> I'm just his Mum. It's my motherly instinct to look after him and to make sure everything's well maintained and pretty, just as if he was at home, where I could look after him. That mother/child bond will always be there. I mean, I gave birth to him and I've got to do what I can for him—and for myself.
>
> *33-year-old, Australian Catholic mother,*
> *bereaved 2 years*

> I come to the cemetery everyday purely because—well, [my wife] and me have been together for close to forty-eight years, so I just want to be with her for a few minutes—no other reasons.
>
> *66-year-old, Maltese Catholic husband,*
> *bereaved 4½ years*

> It's like the only place that I could identify in a physical sense with the last existence of him as a person. That made me understand why people do go to the cemetery. I could never understand why people go all the time; and I still couldn't go all the time. But the people who do go every week, go because they're looking at that place and saying, "That's where that person is; that's where that person lies." And therefore, to visit and see and communicate or contact that person, they must be in that place.
>
> *37-year-old, Australian Jewish sister,*
> *bereaved 8 months*

Maintenance of an emotional bond with the decedent, and this perhaps combined with a sense of duty, becomes most evident on special anniversaries, including those of birth and death, Mothers Day, Fathers Day, various religious festivals such as Christmas, Easter, and some non-Christian religious events. Inclusion of deceased loved ones in these events is of great importance to many mourners.

> I'll go up on birthdays—including my own—because he can't come to my birthday, so I have to go up and see him. I tend to go at Christmas, birthdays and Easter, and those types of things.
>
> *62-year-old, Australian non-religious grandfather,*
> *bereaved 5 years*

I don't feel that I have to go; it's just, I go on special occasions. It seems to have settled down to anniversaries, birthdays and before I'm going away, you know. It's just that I can't buy him presents: because we always exchanged gifts on these occasions.

67-year-old, English Salvation Army wife,
bereaved 4 years

However, not all informants in the study held any concept of an afterlife, nor sought any sense of continuing bond with the decedent. One pragmatic husband was certain that:

If people live after death, they only do so in the minds of the people they leave behind.

62-year-old, Australian non-religious husband,
bereaved 4½ years

SOLACE

More than half of those in the Bereavement Study who were cemetery visitors commented on visiting specifically to seek solace or relief from emotions of grief, and many reported therapeutic benefits from visiting the grave or memorial. It is evident that regular visitation, at least within the first year or so, is very important to many mourners working through personal grief.

For the initial twelve months, I needed to go there and leave flowers and talk to her. I think that helped me in my own personal grieving process.

35-year-old, Australian non-religious
granddaughter, bereaved 4 years

In the morning, I stay there for two hours; then I go home. And if I'm feeling his death, I come back again. It makes me feel much better.

47-year-old, Turkish Muslim mother,
bereaved 14 months

You feel that you need to go because your hurt is still there, but as you start to get your life back together, or back to normality, the pain eases off.

40-year-old, Italian Catholic son, bereaved 3 years

But a single specific anniversary visit may not provide the same cathartic value to that evidently gained by many visitors through their regular visitation.

[My sister's] eldest daughter decided . . . to get married on the anniversary of [her father's] death. The day before my niece's wedding, my husband took my sister out to the cemetery, to sort of help her get through her depression. We thought it might have helped her, but it didn't.

43-year-old, Australian sister-in-law of
eclectic faith, bereaved 3 years

But some mourners, particularly those who may have experienced less emotional upheaval, may not require the solace sought by others from frequent cemetery visitation.

> I don't think going there is significant in the grieving process, in the sense that some people do.
>
> *25-year-old, Australian Catholic grandson,*
> *bereaved 1 year*

Guilt is well recognized as a common grief reaction among many bereaved persons. And several informants mentioned feelings of guilt in relation to not attending as often as they (or others) think they should, and at ending visits. One husband well described his feelings and resolution of such feelings.

> I found that I would be saying to myself, "Oh, God: I haven't been to the cemetery, I'd better go over." I would go as a matter of deliberate intent, because I'd say, "I haven't been." So I'd go and get in the car and I'd drive over there and tidy up around the grave, which served a few purposes. First of all it stopped me feeling guilty, because if I hadn't been there for a while I might feel a bit guilty about it, so I went. . . . I then found that I wasn't feeling guilty about not visiting the grave . . . as other interests in life began to intervene.
>
> *62-year-old, Australian non-religious husband,*
> *bereaved 4½ years*

OTHER REASONS

Several visitors discussed other reasons for going to the cemetery, including taking or accompanying a principal visitor, being in the vicinity with time to spare, inspecting the monument, and visiting out of habit.

Some commented on visiting to take, or accompany, family members or friends:

> I've been to my grandfather's grave about four times since his burial, but only one of those occasions was by myself. The others were to show relatives who had come to town.
>
> *25-year-old, Australian Catholic grandson,*
> *bereaved 1 year*

> Because I mainly visit at [my wife's] prompts, I just respond to her need to go. It's not important for me personally; it's more that I go to support [her]. It's not something that I have to do, and I have no perception of guilt about it: none at all.
>
> *37-year-old, Australian Baptist father,*
> *bereaved 3 years*

Others commented on visiting when they happened to be in the vicinity of the cemetery with some time to spare:

> If I go to town to get pizza by myself, I'll eat it near the cemetery. That's when I sort of think of her . . . if I've got nothing else to do. I've only ever driven in there a few times just to go and see her.
>
> *51-year-old, Australian non-religious husband,*
> *bereaved 2 months*

> I've been . . . a few times recently, probably because we've been in the area making arrangements to move.
>
> *37-year-old, Australian Baptist father,*
> *bereaved 3 years*

A couple of visitors commented on attending specifically to inspect a newly erected monument.

> When I did go by myself, . . . I was just driving past and I thought it was a good time to go in and have a look at the headstone, which I hadn't seen. It was good to see that he's been memorialized in a nice way.
>
> *25-year-old, Australian Catholic grandson,*
> *bereaved 1 year*

And for some mourners, cemetery visitation can evidently become habitual, without necessarily becoming compulsive. A few commented on visiting out of habit.

> At times—and I have felt this on quite a few weekends—we go there just because it's something that we do; it's just become a custom to us.
>
> *27-year-old, Greek Orthodox daughter,*
> *bereaved 4 months*

But others consider habitual visitation may devalue the meaning and importance of visiting a grave or memorial.

> I don't want to ever get used to it to the point where you go every Sunday and wipe it down and clean it: and that's what you do next Sunday as well. I don't want it to become a routine that I just get used to.
>
> *37-year-old, Australian Jewish sister,*
> *bereaved 8 months*

SUMMARY OF VISITATION REASONS

Mourners visit graves and memorials at cemeteries for several reasons. Three principal reasons are to fulfill a perceived sense of obligation, to maintain a significant emotional bond, and to seek solace. These principal reasons appear to be universal, as none was unique to informants of any specific social or cultural identity, and they were identified broadly across a diverse group of general cemetery visitors.

A sense of obligation or duty may be felt towards the decedent, the family, or to the visitor him/herself. It may also relate to the expectations of others, as some mourners feel obliged to visit out of a sense of religious duty, personal respect, or innate compulsion. And a sense of duty or obligation to visit a grave or memorial may be strong enough to compel a mourner to travel considerable distances on specific days to conduct what are often very brief and simple rituals. What may be a self-imposed burden of obligation can evidently become a source of considerable personal stress, which may be best resolved by visiting the cemetery and performing required rituals.

A second principal reason for visiting a cemetery is to maintain or develop an emotional bond with the decedent. Activities such as talking to the decedent, including them in special anniversary days, and leaving gifts at the grave, are evidently very important to many mourners toward maintaining a sense of ongoing relationship.

In noting that relationships are built up through everyday conversation, Walter suggests that it seems likely that if relationships continue after death, this too is likely to entail everyday conversation, either with the dead or about the dead [2]. Such relationships evidently do continue and appear of great importance to many bereaved cemetery visitors.

Within his study of bereavement and health in Australia, Ata found that where emotional ties are deeply rooted in the relationship, they are not easily severed simply because of physical separation. Although not in a cemetery visitation context, Ata also found that attempting to talk to the bereaved was quite common among mourners [3].

The cemetery evidently provides an important physical location for many mourners to either escape from or pass through the anguish of bereavement. To many, being present at the grave or memorial site is essential toward maintaining a vital emotional bond.

The third principal reason for visiting a cemetery is specifically to seek solace from one's personal grief, including relief from the feelings of guilt. Some of the guilt commonly experienced may be due to not fulfilling a perceived obligation or duty to visit, or it may relate to neglect of the relationship. So, at least within early bereavement, regular cemetery visitation is evidently of significant therapeutic benefit to many mourners seeking to work through intense grief. And visiting a grave can provide a perception of being with the decedent, and a sense of the decedent's presence can provide appreciable solace from the common early-bereavement anxiety of separation.

Having now briefly reviewed the main reasons why mourners actually visit cemeteries, in the next chapter we will explore the most common gravesite activities of visitors.

REFERENCES

1. P. Bachelor, *Cemetery visitation: The place of the cemetery in the grief process,* unpublished Ph.D. thesis, Charles Sturt University, Wagga Wagga, 2001.
2. J. A. Walter, *The revival of death,* Routledge, London, 1994.
3. A. W. Ata, *Bereavement & health in Australia: Gender, psychological, religious and cross-cultural issues,* David Lovell, Melbourne, 1994.

CHAPTER 9
Visitation Activities

The previous chapter introduced the main reasons why mourners visit cemeteries. In this chapter, we will identify the most popular activities of cemetery visitors, and seek to understand, from the perspectives of various mourners, personal interpretations of the meanings of their main activities.

Cemetery visitation activities are here defined as either the physical or mental actions performed by visitors within a cemetery, and in association with a specific grave or memorial. The Bereavement Study revealed three principal gravesite activities, two secondary activities, and several apparently less-common activities among cemetery visitors [1].

The identified principal activities are: placing flowers, maintaining the grave or memorial, and talking to the decedent. Crying and prayer appear as somewhat less-common or secondary activities, and several other activities are identified as occurring even less still.

PLACING FLOWERS

The vast majority of visitors advised that they commonly bring and place flowers when visiting the grave or memorial. However, not all bring flowers on every occasion. Some visitors choose to place flowers only occasionally, and some who visit several times each week feel no need to replace flowers on each visit.

But either ensuring that fresh flowers are maintained on the grave at all times, or at least placing new flowers on every visit, was reported by most visiting mourners. And all but one of these informants were female.

> When we come together, we stop first at the florist . . . All the flowers get taken out of the vase and the good ones separated from the bad. The two of us do our flowers together and that probably takes about an hour; I'm pretty fussy. I've become a little bit of a flower arranger since all this has happened and a bit fussy about how it looks.
>
> *27-year-old, Australian Catholic mother, bereaved 10 months*

Mum always believed in fresh flowers, so we bring her fresh flowers. Dad buys them on Friday, because he goes to the market then.

> *27-year-old, Greek Orthodox daughter,*
> *bereaved 4 months*

However, several male visitors advised that they also bring and place fresh flowers on the grave or memorial, but not on each visit.

I took flowers out of our own garden for a while, but not the last few times.

> *51-year-old, Australian non-religious husband,*
> *bereaved 2 months*

Although many cemeteries do not permit them, some infrequent visitors prefer to use artificial flowers. The use of artificial flowers can be viewed both positively and negatively.

Because we can't be there regularly, we tend to change silk flowers once every few months. We get plenty of nice silk flowers; we won't take live ones, because we just don't want dead looking flowers.

> *37-year-old, Australian Baptist father,*
> *bereaved 3 years*

I always buy flowers. . . . One time—I got so annoyed—my mother actually took bloody plastic flowers there. I chucked them away and told her I didn't see them; they must have blown away or something. . . . After about twelve months, they'd been really weather-beaten and they looked awful. I didn't want to look at them. I thought, "No, Grandma deserves better than that."

> *35-year-old, Australian non-religious*
> *granddaughter, bereaved 4 years*

Though several female visitors commented on also tending other graves or memorials while at the cemetery, no males reported giving any attention to those of people unknown to them.

My daughter . . . likes to visit the children's section too on the way down, and if there's no flowers on one, she'll take some from what we've got and she'll put it there: yes. "Poor thing; they've got no flowers."

> *47-year-old, Australian daughter of no specific*
> *faith, bereaved 5 months*

And at least one widow appreciated a friend tending her husband's grave for her when she had been unable to perform her routine task.

I . . . put some fresh flowers every week. . . . Even when I was really ill, I had someone place fresh flowers on his grave.

> *70-year-old, Italian Catholic wife, bereaved 3 years*

While to many visitors placing flowers is a sign of respect, or a symbolic gift to the decedent, not everyone fully understands their reasons for placing flowers.

I take flowers every time I visit . . . but it's only a ritual; it's got no significance that I can think of.

67-year-old, English Salvation Army wife,
bereaved 4 years

Only two visitors in the study advised that they do not bring and place flowers
on any occasion; both were male, and neither saw any value in flowers.

I certainly wouldn't put flowers there. I don't think that's significant or
necessary.

25-year-old, Australian Catholic grandson, bereaved 1 year

MAINTAINING THE GRAVE OR MEMORIAL

Two-thirds of the visitors in the Bereavement Study advised that they
engage in some form of routine maintenance activity to the plaque or monument,
or lawn or garden relating to the grave. Several spoke of their own need to clean
the plaque or monument.

I just trim the grass around the concrete base of the bronze plaque. My
next-door neighbour told me that the way to keep the bronze plaque up is
with a bit of baby oil rubbed into a rag. I've also got an old toothbrush, which
I use to get into the lettering and what-have-you, just to make it look neat,
clean and tidy.

62-year-old, Australian non-religious husband,
bereaved 4½ years

Once a week, I wipe down the monument. I get a small bucket to carry the
water, but I usually have a damp cloth.

66-year-old, Maltese Catholic husband,
bereaved 4½ years

Several visitors advised that they also maintain the lawn or garden covering
or adjoining the grave, even though they recognize that it may not be technically
necessary. Performing some maintenance activity on the grave or monument
provides an important sense of satisfaction to mourners as they either fulfill a duty
of care and/or demonstrate continuing love for the decedent.

All I can do is trim her grass and do her flowers, so I'm more than happy
to make sure that I do that, because here is my outlet for mothering. . . . This
is the place where I can do things for her. So it's very important to me that
I am able to do those things for her, you know: very important. . . . We know
the gardeners do the borders and everything, but it gives us great satisfaction
in trimming back all the little bits of grass, you know.

27-year-old, Australian Catholic mother,
bereaved 10 months

And some visiting mourners advised that they always carry toolkits in their cars, specifically for maintaining their respective plaques, monuments and surrounds.

> I keep everything in my car boot, like scissors for the flowers and to cut the grass. I fertilize the lawn, clean the headstone and put pretty windmills on there.
>
> *33-year-old, Australian Catholic mother,*
> *bereaved 2 years*

Nevertheless, not all visitors feel any compulsion to perform some maintenance activity within the cemetery.

> The place is immaculate, so I didn't need to do anything.
>
> *25-year-old, Australian Catholic grandson,*
> *bereaved 1 year*

TALKING TO THE DECEDENT

More than half of the visiting mourners in the Bereavement Study mentioned that they commonly talk to the decedent at the grave or memorial site. These conversations may be brief, such as just saying hello and assuring the decedent that they are missed, or they may involve updating the decedent on recent and current events. Some conversations, particularly at infrequent visits, may be quite lengthy.

Several visitors specifically spoke of updating the decedent on recent and current events.

> I talk to her about the past and what's going on in my life: a bit of an update on what's happening and what all the others are doing, because I know they don't visit. I remember telling her when my younger cousin had her second child: a little girl. I remember telling her that she looks like this, she's nothing like that and it's a shame that you weren't here. You know, just a bit of a gossip session really: one way.
>
> *35-year-old, Australian non-religious*
> *granddaughter, bereaved 4 years*

Some visitors specifically reported that they always renew their acquaintance by saying hello and assuring the deceased that they are missed and not forgotten.

> I just look at Dad's photo and say a few words: that I miss him and I'm still thinking of him, and for him to look after us. . . . Even if I don't drop in to the cemetery, every time I go past or drive anywhere near it, I just can't help but say, "Good day, Dad. How are you going? I hope you're well."
>
> *40-year-old, Italian Catholic son, bereaved 3 years*

And visitors of some faiths ask their deceased to intercede on behalf of family members.

> I talk to [my wife] about how things are going. And when someone is sick from the family, I just ask her to pray for them.
>
> *66-year-old, Maltese Catholic husband,*
> *bereaved 4½ years*

Still other visitors considered that their graveside talks were not specifically notable and were just of a general or non-specific nature.

> I talk to [my husband], . . . but not about anything in particular, because I can talk to him anytime.
>
> *67-year-old, English Salvation Army wife,*
> *bereaved 4 years*

Nevertheless, despite its evident popularity as a specific grave or memorial site activity, not all visiting mourners do engage in any talk to their deceased.

> I don't think either of us does.
>
> *37-year-old, Australian Baptist father,*
> *bereaved 3 years*

CRYING

Although common at funerals, and more prevalent during initial stages of grief, the emotional release of crying generally becomes less common over subsequent visits, as mourners accommodate their loss and modify their responses. Almost half of all visiting mourners in the Bereavement Study spoke of crying in relation to visiting the respective grave or memorial site.

> Usually, I come here crying and leave feeling better.
>
> *27-year-old, Australian Catholic mother,*
> *bereaved 10 months*

> I should have stopped driving there, because I was starting to get dangerous. I wouldn't stop crying. The crying went on for two and a half years; I was a mess.
>
> *62-year-old, Australian non-religious*
> *grandfather, bereaved 5 years*

Some informants recognized crying to be less common among modern Anglo-based cultures and more prevalent among other traditional European cultures, including Greek and Italian.

> The Italian way of crying and all this—and they carry on a little bit—is a way of letting it all out; it helps to cleanse. The Anglo-Saxon way of just being polite keeps the grief still going on.
>
> *40-year-old, Italian Catholic son,*
> *bereaved 3 years*

But at least one Anglo-Australian informant considered the crying of others within the cemetery to be intrusive and offensive to her.

> If I'm visiting the cemetery and someone else is bawling their eyes out and screaming, I think it's offensive, because they're intruding on my grieving. To me, that's not true bereavement: it's just an act. I really hate that. It seems to me, that women who cry the loudest think they're the ones who grieve the most. But neither do I think that they should have to hide their grieving. I mean, if you want to cry: cry!
>
> *34-year-old, Australian Anglican*
> *de facto wife, bereaved 3 years*

While several males mentioned a "lump in the throat" or a "tear in the eye," only one admitted to regular crying at the gravesite. One husband specifically mentioned that he and his sons intentionally withheld their emotions.

> Initially some memories were quite painful, but . . . I didn't show it; to do so would be a sign of weakness. . . . The three of us are not the type to show our emotions, particularly in that way. We would by nature try to conceal our emotions.
>
> *62-year-old, Australian non-religious*
> *husband, bereaved 4½ years*

However, while withholding emotions may be more common among males, it is not unique to that sex.

> I never actually sat there and had a bit of a cry. I've always been sitting there talking to her. Is that a bad thing? It's just who I am; I don't cry.
>
> *35-year-old, Australian non-religious*
> *granddaughter, bereaved 4 years*

PRAYER

Although not as popular as placing flowers, maintaining the grave or memorial, and talking to the decedent, prayer is another moderately common activity among some cemetery visitors. Two-thirds of visitors in the Bereavement Study professed holding a religious faith, and almost half of these people advised that they pray at the grave or memorial site.

> In visiting them, I also pray for them, so that sort of helps us to communicate in a spiritual way. . . . I pray pretty much the same at the gravesite as I do away from the cemetery.
>
> *27-year-old, Greek Orthodox daughter,*
> *bereaved 4 months*

> In visiting him and praying for him, we feel like he's next to us. While we're visiting, we feel close to God too, because we're praying for him there, you know.
>
> *52-year-old, Turkish Muslim father,*
> *bereaved 14 months*

But some otherwise religious visitors specifically stated that they do not pray at the grave or memorial site.

> I don't say any prayers or anything like that.
>> *40-year-old, Italian Catholic son, bereaved 3 years*

OTHER ACTIVITIES

Several other gravesite activities were found to appear less often within the Bereavement Study than did the above principal and secondary activities. Other activities identified from the study include performing various religious rites, kissing the memorial, feasting or drinking with the decedent, placing gifts or ornaments, silent contemplation, talking with other mourners, and imagining the decedent.

One regular visitor and her husband reported that she maintains a logbook in which she records details of all subsequent burials in the respective cemetery compartment.

Several mourners of different faiths referred to various religious rites, including blessing the grave, consecrating the monument, symbolic feasting, playing recorded scripture readings, and burning incense.

> Blessing the grave is usually done on a Saturday. The priest will come to the cemetery where we'd be waiting for him at the grave. He prays for her soul and we have a bowl of boiled wheat with raisins, sugar and almonds mixed in, and that symbolizes the body of the deceased. The priest blesses the wheat and then once it's all over, we just have a bit of the wheat and a biscuit, or whatever anybody else brings along. We spend a bit of time there with the deceased and then they usually all come over to the house and have a coffee.
>> *27-year-old, Greek Orthodox daughter,*
>> *bereaved 4 months*

> The monument is being organized at the moment, and next month we will have it consecrated by a rabbi and we'll all probably go to the cemetery.
>> *37-year-old, Australian Jewish sister,*
>> *bereaved 8 months*

A few socially and culturally-diverse mourners advised that on each visit they always kiss the memorial.

> My first reaction is to kiss the stone.
>> *40-year-old, Italian Catholic son,*
>> *bereaved 3 years*

> I never, ever go away without giving [his] headstone a kiss.
>> *60-year-old, Australian non-religious*
>> *grandmother, bereaved 5 years*

Some visitors have gained considerable personal benefit from communicating with other sympathetic mourners at the cemetery, with whom they can share legitimate understanding. Self-help mothers' cooperatives have developed naturally at specific children's areas within some larger cemeteries.

> In talking to other mums that have lost kids, we've developed a great bond, because we're all going through the same thing. In some ways, it's more helpful than talking to a counselor who's gone through textbooks, but hasn't gone through our emotions and how hard it is. So yes, a lot of us mums have become quite close. Other people just wouldn't understand us; they'd think we've gone nuts.
>
> *33-year-old, Australian Catholic mother,*
> *bereaved 2 years*

> A lot of our conversations are what you'd call "bitch sessions," if you overheard us. They're just about all the stupid things that people say to us, and how our families make us feel, and stupid things our best friends say. It's really good to have that outlet, because otherwise it could fester. So the lack of understanding is one of the big things we talk about.
>
> *27-year-old, Australian Catholic mother,*
> *bereaved 10 months*

A couple of male visitors in the study related humorous incidents in which they had poured out drink over the grave.

> It's a funny thing I know, but I was there probably only a couple of days after the funeral and there were these two bottles of wine that she just wouldn't let me open. I don't know why; they were nothing special—just two bottles of plonk—but she just wouldn't let me open them, for no reason at all. So I went down and opened those bottles of wine and poured them all over her grave. I had a mouthful of each and threw the bottles in the rubbish bin. Why I did that, I don't know, but I couldn't drink them after that. One bottle wasn't bad actually; it was a waste.
>
> *51-year-old, Australian non-religious husband,*
> *bereaved 2 months*

SUMMARY OF VISITATION ACTIVITIES

The principal gravesite activities of most mourners are identified as placing flowers, maintaining the grave or memorial, and talking to the decedent. Crying and praying generally occur less frequently, while several other activities were identified as being undertaken by fewer people still.

Placing flowers at the grave or memorial appears to be the most popular gravesite activity among people of diverse faiths and relationships to decedents, with over 90% of visitors in the study advising that they place flowers at the cemetery.

Maintaining the grave or memorial is another particularly popular visitation activity. Just as the placement of flowers may symbolize a gift, so maintenance of the grave may symbolize continuing care for a decedent. Almost 70% of visitors advised that they perform some maintenance activities at the grave or memorial site.

Talking to a decedent at the grave or memorial site is yet another popular activity of cemetery visitors across various faiths and relationships, though such communication would seem to require some personal concept of an afterlife. Over 50% of visitors in the study mentioned that they do talk to the decedent at the cemetery. Common gravesite conversations include regular courtesies and renewal of acquaintance, assuring the decedent that they are missed and not forgotten, and updating the decedent on recent and current events. Some visitors also ask the decedent to intercede on behalf of, or care for, other family members.

Crying and prayer are moderately common activities. Crying is more evident during early stages of grief, among females and those of Southern European origin. Gravesite prayer is a relatively common practice among some religious visitors.

Other visitor activities include performing various religious rites, kissing the memorial, feasting or drinking with the decedent, placing mementos and other gifts on the grave, standing silently at the memorial site, talking with other mourners, and conjuring up images of the decedent.

Consciously or not, it appears that cemetery visitation activities serve at least one of two purposes. These purposes are: to enable mourners to undertake perceived duties and fulfill their obligations, and to maintain a significant emotional bond with the decedent. Undertaking perceived duties and fulfilling obligations were reported to be helpful toward mitigating the common bereavement emotion of guilt. Maintaining an emotional bond with the decedent was found to be helpful toward mitigating other bereavement emotions, including grief, sadness, loss, and loneliness.

This concludes the review of cemetery visitation activities. The next chapter introduces the main emotional experiences of visitors.

REFERENCE

1. P. Bachelor, *Cemetery visitation: The place of the cemetery in the grief process,* unpublished Ph.D. thesis, Charles Sturt University, Wagga Wagga, 2001.

CHAPTER 10
Emotions

In the previous chapter, we reviewed major cemetery visitation activities. In this one, we now identify and examine key emotional experiences of visitors.

Emotion is a somewhat elusive concept to define, but it relates to potentially intense internal feelings. It is considered to involve a construction of cognitive, physiological, and behavioral components. The cognitive component involves a subjective conscious experience; the physiological component involves bodily arousal; and the behavioral component involves characteristic overt expressions [1].

Cemetery visitation emotions are here defined as significant internal feelings (bodily arousal) and specific responses (overt expressions) experienced by visitors in association with attending a specific grave or memorial of a deceased significant other (the subjective conscious experience).

Emotional theorists identify at least eight primary emotions, and propose that additional emotions are produced by blends of primary emotions and variations in intensity. According to Plutchik, emotions such as grief, sadness and pensiveness involve one primary emotion, though experienced at different levels of intensity [2].

Several specific emotions relating to cemetery visitation were revealed in the recent Bereavement Study. The most closely related of these emotions were then clustered into two major groups, or primary emotions, which are here identified as "Sorrow" and "Solace." So two major groups, or primary emotions, and six other specific emotions of cemetery visitors are here recognized and discussed in descending order of their frequency of occurrence within the study [3].

The identified emotions of bereaved cemetery visitors were: sorrow (including grief and sadness), solace (including relief and peace), guilt, respect, loss, loneliness, fear, and anger.

Of course, each person's bereavement response is a unique individual experience. Even the emotional responses of two parents concurrently mourning their loss of the same child usually vary significantly.

It's difficult, in the sense that everyone grieves differently. Just because I was her Mum and he was her Dad, doesn't mean that we're grieving in the same way. I found that I went through real anger. . . . At the same time, he was still just crying and sad. He couldn't understand why I was so angry. So you go through these different phases differently.

27-year-old, Australian Catholic mother,
bereaved 10 months

In fact, all visitors in the study indicated that they experienced various emotions at different times, and most reported experiencing emotions of both sorrow and solace. Emotions of both major groups were often experienced within a specific visitation pattern, and were occasionally experienced in association with the same visit, such as displacing initial sorrow with solace.

It is also apparent that most of the emotions expressed are not necessarily exclusive of each other, as seemingly contradictory emotions may be simultaneously experienced in relation to separate, but concurrent issues of bereavement and visitation. For example, a visitor may feel sadness at their loss, or guilt at not visiting frequently, but pleasure at being able to arrange flowers, and a sense of peace with the memorial environment.

SORROW

Sorrow is one of the primary emotions identified in the study, and is here defined as emotional distress in response to loss. As a group of emotions, sorrow includes grief (including anguish and despair) and sadness (including pensiveness). Most mourners in the study referred to sorrow emotions in relation to visiting a grave or memorial.

Sadness is a state of unhappiness, which is considered to be less intense and severe than grief. At the more intense end of the sorrow spectrum, grief may be characterized by a greater degree of emotional pain and anxiety.

Sadness was the most common cemetery visitation emotion found within the sorrow group, and the most frequently expressed of all emotions.

The cemetery is . . . a place of sadness: quite a bit of grieving, of course.

27-year-old, Greek Orthodox daughter,
bereaved 4 months

I feel just sadness and loss.

64-year-old, Australian Uniting mother,
bereaved 3 years

I feel very sad, of course. . . . When I go, I remember when we were together, but now I really feel sad when I go to the cemetery. Now I go to see my brother in the grave, and that is very, very sad too.

66-year-old, Italian Catholic wife,
bereaved 5 years

Displaying the optimistic hallmark of successful survivors, some informants expressed a greater sadness for others than for their own situation.

> I guess the cemetery is a sad place, not because [my wife's] buried there, but because of some of the other people you see come there. Like, there's a little old lady who just sits there; she's done this nice little garden and she just sits there for hours on end. She brings a cup of tea and dinner. That's sad—not that it's a particularly sad place.
>
> *51-year-old, Australian non-religious husband,*
> *bereaved 2 months*

> There is a sense of sadness when you see a plaque with somebody that's young. . . . I feel sad when I see a little person that's died.
>
> *67-year-old, English Salvation Army wife,*
> *bereaved 4 years*

Grief was another frequently expressed emotion within the sorrow group, and several mourners discussed feelings of anguish in association with cemetery visits. Those still experiencing anguish at the times of interviews had been bereaved within recent months, while others referred to their earlier experiences.

> It is a really, really hard thing: a heart wrenching experience to go.
>
> *37-year-old, Australian Jewish sister,*
> *bereaved 8 months*

But fortunately, within most bereavement experiences, early grief normally subsides to the less intense emotion of sadness.

> I used to stress something shocking; it really knocked me around. And when I stopped just dropping into the place, I improved quicker. I could have quite easily said, "That's it; I'm not going any more." That's how it was stressing me, but I was determined not to let it stress me to the point that I wouldn't go.
>
> *62-year-old, Australian non-religious*
> *grandfather, bereaved 5 years*

One female mourner in the study had been under psychiatric care for three years following a significant death, and several others had undergone months of bereavement counseling. However, only half of those who had tried professional counseling reported it to have been beneficial. A few women had also tried antidepressant drugs, but only one person in the study reported their drug therapy to have proved beneficial.

> I had a mental breakdown . . . I think it was [my brother-in-law's] death that actually popped it. . . . I just went and fell off the top as soon as I heard about the accident. . . . My breakdown has been very, very difficult for my immediate family. My husband . . . thought I should just snap out of it. Most people think, "Well, OK; so you're depressed. Now get

better." But it's like a disease; mental illness *is* a disease and you can't snap out of it.

43-year-old, Australian sister-in-law of
eclectic faith, bereaved 3 years

I had to go to the doctor and was put on medication for depression for about six months.

45-year-old, Australian non-religious female
secret-lover, bereaved 3 years

But even though sorrow was the most discussed set of emotions, three male informants reported that they did not experience any sorrow when visiting the cemetery.

For me, it's a location where we buried our daughter and . . . that's important; but in terms of it bringing things back to me, or heightening emotional responses, it doesn't.

37-year-old, Australian Baptist father,
bereaved 3 years

One male visitor, having retired from an active military career, revealed his personal need to conceal any intrinsic emotions of sorrow.

Initially some memories were quite painful, but because of the inherent discipline that my previous occupation engenders, I didn't show it; to do so would be a sign of weakness.

62-year-old, Australian non-religious husband,
bereaved 4½ years

And another informant considered that his emotional feelings at the cemetery were largely the product of his own thoughts at the time.

Sometimes I feel a little bit of sadness at the cemetery, and other times I have a laugh and chuckle; it depends on what I think about at the time. If you think about a good time you sort of laugh and chuckle, but if you're thinking about sad things then you will be sad.

51-year-old, Australian non-religious
husband, bereaved 2 months

SOLACE

The second primary emotion identified in the study is that of solace, which is here defined as a state of comfort or relief from distress, attained by soothing and consoling. The solace group of emotions includes relief and peace.

Seeking solace was also identified as one of the principal reasons for cemetery visitation, with almost as many mourners referring to emotions of solace in relation to visiting a grave or memorial as mentioned sorrow.

Relief was the more frequently expressed specific emotion of solace, with more than half of all visitors referring to feelings of relief or comfort.

> Once I get there, I feel happy: quite happy. . . . Just bringing the fresh flowers and things gives me a good feeling.
>
> *70-year-old, Italian Catholic wife,*
> *bereaved 3 years*

> I come here because it brings me comfort.
>
> *27-year-old, Australian Catholic mother,*
> *bereaved 10 months*

> On the way to the cemetery, I feel happy that I'm going to see him. I just can't wait to come and say hello to him. But when I'm leaving I do feel sad.
>
> *33-year-old, Australian Catholic mother,*
> *bereaved 2 years*

And some comfort may be drawn from the specific location or cemetery compartment visited, or from the concept of others being present.

> If she can't be with me, then I am just so relieved that she's in that area with all the other children. I can speak on behalf of probably fifteen different sets of parents that I've met down there. It brings us all so much comfort to know they're all together: it really does.
>
> *27-year-old, Australian Catholic mother,*
> *bereaved 10 months*

> At first, I used to worry about him being up at the cemetery by himself . . . but then I started to think, "You're somewhere else now with other people." And he isn't by himself: definitely. My uncle is with him and so is my Mum. That's how I comfort myself. I don't think about whether it's true or not.
>
> *60-year-old, Australian non-religious*
> *grandmother, bereaved 5 years*

But not all mourners experience any particular sense of comfort from visiting the cemetery.

> There are no happy memories in the cemetery.
>
> *37-year-old, Australian Jewish sister,*
> *bereaved 8 months*

Peace was another popularly expressed emotion of solace, with more than half of all visitors referring to a sense of peace pertaining to the cemetery environment.

> Within the cemetery, I definitely feel a sense of peace—just peaceful. It's a peaceful sort of quiet place. It's a very beautiful landscape actually— a very nice place to look at.
>
> *25-year-old, Australian Catholic*
> *grandson, bereaved 1 year*

I'm at ease when I'm at the cemetery; it's a peaceful place.

47-year-old, Australian daughter of no specific
faith, bereaved 5 months

But one's perception of any peace at the cemetery may relate to the mode of death, and the mourner's relationship to the decedent. The mother of a young woman who died in a car accident said:

The cemetery is nice, but I don't feel any sense of peace with her; with my father and mother I do, but not with my daughter.

64-year-old, Australian Uniting mother,
bereaved 3 years

Others spoke of progressive emotional transitions, as their intensity of grief subsided and a sense of peace progressively emerged.

The scenery has become progressively more and more peaceful. . . . Initially, I found that instead of giving solace, going there tended to make me remember the immediacy of the funeral . . . it brought it all back.

62-year-old, Australian non-religious
husband, bereaved 4½ years

Not always so, but lately I feel peaceful. . . . I'm quite happy to be there now.

60-year-old, Australian non-religious
grandmother, bereaved 5 years

As with relief, a sense of peace may also be drawn from the specific location or cemetery compartment visited.

I don't find the cemetery to be sad or depressing in any way. . . . It's a focal point that just brings it all together and it's peaceful. There is a sense of peace there, certainly at the mausoleum. That's peaceful; it really is.

40-year-old, Italian Catholic son,
bereaved 3 years

[The children's area] is a very different area in that it certainly brings the parents a lot of peace and a lot of comfort; and I know cemeteries are probably meant to do that anyway, but I find it a lot more in that area.

27-year-old, Australian Catholic
mother, bereaved 10 months

But unfortunately, not all mourners experience any sense of peace when visiting the grave or memorial of a deceased loved one.

It is not in any way peaceful. The cemetery can be peaceful because it's quiet, but it's not peaceful in that particular place.

37-year-old, Australian Jewish sister,
bereaved 8 months

GUILT

Several mourners in the study mentioned feelings of guilt in relation to visiting the grave or memorial, and most of the guilt experienced related to one's frequency of visitation.

> I felt really relieved the last time I went, because I felt so guilty that I hadn't been for a while.
>
> *35-year-old, Australian non-religious*
> *granddaughter, bereaved 4 years*

Individual mourners also experienced guilt at not feeling distressed, and at leaving the deceased.

> I think it's peaceful. I feel possibly a trifle guilty because I'm relaxed there.
>
> *62-year-old, Australian non-religious*
> *husband, bereaved 4½ years*

> Now, . . . I just cry walking back to the car, and I think it's because I feel guilty about leaving him there.
>
> *45-year-old, Australian non-religious female*
> *secret-lover, bereaved 3 years*

But one mourner questioned the logic of his own perception of guilt.

> If I hadn't been there for a while I might feel a bit guilty about it, so I went. Now, who the hell I would feel guilty to is another matter, because who the hell would know? The dead don't: and the kids hardly ever go there. It's like a reflex. I think that is interesting. Well, why the bloody-hell should I feel guilty?
>
> *62-year-old, Australian non-religious*
> *husband, bereaved 4½ years*

And some informants reported no feelings of guilt at not visiting the cemetery.

> It's not important for me personally. . . . It's not something that I have to do, and I have no perception of guilt about it: none at all.
>
> *37-year-old, Australian Baptist father,*
> *bereaved 3 years*

One mourner expressed her opinion that appropriately-founded guilt might exacerbate grief in some people.

> I didn't feel guilty after he'd died. I really believe that people grieve a long time, or grieve excessively, because of guilt. That's what I believe. But I did everything I could for him that I thought was appropriate.
>
> *34-year-old, Australian Anglican*
> *de facto wife, bereaved 3 years*

LOSS

All but one person in the study had experienced a significant degree of loss in relation to their respective bereavement, and all but one other had some previous experience of loss through the death of another close family member. However, most considered that their previous loss experience did not adequately prepare and assist them in coping with their more recent and more significant bereavement.

Only a third of visiting mourners referred specifically to the emotion of loss in relation to visiting the grave or memorial.

> I feel just sadness and loss.
>
> *64-year-old, Australian Uniting mother,*
> *bereaved 3 years*

The emotion of loss within the cemetery is evidently influenced by several variables, including the personality of the bereaved, relationship of the decedent, circumstances of the death, and the duration of bereavement.

> I don't think that everybody understands . . . the individual situation every time. Just because you can lose a grandparent and go to a funeral and be back at work tomorrow, doesn't mean that I'm going to survive the loss of my cat. You know, it depends on the person and on the importance of the relationship. Every situation is so totally different: you function differently.
>
> *37-year-old, Australian Jewish sister,*
> *bereaved 8 months*

> The loss of a loved one is horrible no matter who it is, but I know that the loss of a child is worse than losing my brother. I understand the cemetery has to treat everyone as being in the same position. The last thing you can do is say, "Well they lost their child and you only lost your husband." I mean, you can't do that to people.
>
> *27-year-old, Australian Catholic mother,*
> *bereaved 10 months*

RESPECT

Several mourners in the study referred specifically to the emotion of respect, in relation to visiting the grave or memorial. A person may feel respect toward one or more decedents, to all of the deceased within a cemetery, to other mourners, or toward the concept of the cemetery itself.

To many mourners, the cemetery is symbolic of humanity's respect for its dead.

> The cemetery is emblematic of the respect with which we held the people who are there. It marks us as a civilized society, in that we show respect by honoring that memory. . . . I would suspect that respect for the dead and those things which are emblematic of that respect—which obviously includes cemeteries—is common to all, and I think it distinguishes the human animal

from others. . . . A cemetery should be treated with the same respect that the people who are there should be treated with, if they were still alive.

62-year-old, Australian non-religious husband,
bereaved 4½ years

I guess it's a respect: a respect for the place as a final resting-place.

37-year-old, Australian Jewish sister,
bereaved 8 months

Several mourners considered that their visitation was demonstrative of respect for the decedent.

I feel that he feels I'm there: that I'm showing respect.

40-year-old, Italian Catholic son,
bereaved 3 years

But not everyone feels that cemetery visitation is essential for this purpose.

I don't find that it is a lack of respect not to go there.

37-year-old, Australian Jewish sister,
bereaved 8 months

One frequent visitor recognized that differing concepts of appropriate respect can be problematic.

I know different people view respect differently and that's a problem in the cemetery. Some people think it shows a lack of respect to leave so many things around. I suppose to everyone it's different—it's in the eye of the beholder.

27-year-old, Australian Catholic mother,
bereaved 10 months

FEAR

Some visitors reported occasional experiences of fear in relation to cemetery visitation. Fear may relate to the unknown, the deceased, or to personal feelings of vulnerability.

Mum used to take us to visit [my grandparents' grave] about once a month. I still remember going to that cemetery. I used to be scared to tread on the graves; I used to jump over them all the time.

34-year-old, Australian Anglican
de facto wife, bereaved 3 years

I guess, sometimes I feel scared and I look over my shoulder, but most times, I feel happy: just that he knows I'm there.

33-year-old, Australian Catholic mother,
bereaved 2 years

But a greater proportion of visitors specifically advised that they do not feel any fear when visiting the cemetery.

> The cemetery is a peaceful place; I don't ever feel frightened.
>
> *67-year-old, English Salvation Army wife,*
> *bereaved 4 years*

LONELINESS

Some mourners in the study mentioned the emotion of loneliness, or missing the decedent, in relation to visiting the grave or memorial.

> At the cemetery . . . I remember it's a love and I am alone.
>
> *66-year-old, Italian Catholic wife,*
> *bereaved 5 years*

> I talk to him, you know, about everything. I tell him I miss him.
>
> *47-year-old, Turkish Muslim mother,*
> *bereaved 14 months*

ANGER

A couple of individuals in the study referred to the emotion of anger in relation to visiting the grave or memorial. In one case, the mourner's anger was expressed toward the decedent, while another's was toward non-visiting family members.

> I think it has become easier to visit these days . . . But I get angry at him too— more than anything because he's actually died. He had so much to live for.
>
> *45-year-old, Australian non-religious female*
> *secret-lover, bereaved 3 years*

> I used to have terrible arguments with the others, because they never went. Even if I rang them up and said I was going and I'd offer to pick them up, they wouldn't want to come for the drive. "Too busy!" I get so angry with them. . . . I get so annoyed with the rest of the family, because the bastards never go.
>
> *35-year-old, Australian non-religious*
> *granddaughter, bereaved 4 years*

EMOTIONAL CHANGE

More than half of all visitors in the study referred to a process of gradual change in their emotions in relation to visiting the grave or memorial. Unpleasant emotions, such as those of sorrow (including grief and sadness), guilt, loss, loneliness, and anger, were all found to progressively subside in most regular visitors.

My emotions have got better. At first, visiting was more difficult: it was very, very emotional. That has got a bit better now; I definitely feel better.

70-year-old, Italian Catholic wife,
bereaved 3 years

I don't get as upset now. I suppose you'd say I find it easier to visit these days.

64-year-old, Australian Uniting mother,
bereaved 3 years

One visiting mourner well described what he saw as a logical process of emotional change.

What has happened progressively is that a sense of logic began to take over from the emotions. And logic says that underneath the ground is a coffin, in which is what's left of the body, and that's all. Therefore, . . . there's not the emotionalism that there was initially.

62-year-old, Australian non-religious
husband, bereaved 4½ years

And the same person was surprised at the rate of his own emotional change.

I recall a tremendous sense of loss at first, when she died. Although I was surprised and even felt somewhat guilty about the rapidity at which I seemed to get over it.

62-year-old, Australian non-religious
husband, bereaved 4½ years

Another informant noted that acceptance and emotional change might be expected to differ, depending on the relationship to the decedent.

It's amazing how it has changed. I think you accept it and make it part of your life; it's happened and you move on. I think it's also got a lot to do with personality and the make up of a person, because my mother still gets very emotional when she goes. But she's the wife; it's a different grief experience.

40-year-old, Italian Catholic son,
bereaved 3 years

But subsidence in emotions of distress following the death of someone significant does not always occur, and resignation to such a loss may take several weeks, months, or years; or might never fully occur with some mourners. And several people in the study indicated that in having difficulty accommodating a significant death, they, friends or family members, tend to avoid the cemetery.

One of my daughters—the eldest one—doesn't go to the grave very often, because even though four years have passed now, she still doesn't accept the death of her mother, but the other one she goes every Sunday.

66-year-old, Maltese Catholic husband,
bereaved 4½ years

We don't need to go all the time, you know; and our younger daughter doesn't like to go at all. She'll go if we want her to come with us, but she doesn't really like it and won't go on her own.

64-year-old, Australian Uniting mother,
bereaved 3 years

[A friend's] son got killed in a car accident; he was only twenty-one. I don't think the father has even been to the cemetery since the funeral; that was ten years ago. He won't talk about it, like it just didn't happen, except that his son is not there.

62-year-old, Australian non-religious
grandfather, bereaved 5 years

Only one regular visitor advised that she was still experiencing some difficulty in coming to terms with the reality of her loss.

I do have bad days; I can go there and just cry. I suppose I'll just never accept that he's gone.

33-year-old, Australian Catholic mother,
bereaved 2 years

Attig recognizes that some people choose to remain in grief for fear that if they stop longing for those they have lost they will stop loving them [4]. Some mourners are concerned that any subsidence in their grief may equate to a subsidence in their love.

It is a really, really hard thing: a heart wrenching experience to go. I don't want it ever to change from that. I don't want to ever be able to walk up to his gravesite and not cry, and not feel, and not hurt.

37-year-old, Australian Jewish sister,
bereaved 8 months

I'm not trying to rebuild my life in any way. . . . I don't see any future. There's no future without him: no future at all. I can't build a new life without him: I can't. . . . Every night when I go to bed I pray, "Please don't let me wake up in the morning," and the next morning I say, "Oh God, I'm still here; now I have to live through another day." I am very interested in assisted suicide; I think I'd like that, but I guess I'm probably a coward at heart.

75-year-old, Australian Catholic wife,
bereaved 14 months

Some features of grief are known to continue for years after a loss, and some aspects of grief-work may never end for some mourners [5]. One father well recognized that while his grief emotions may have subsided, they have certainly not ceased.

We don't feel perhaps quite as emotional as we did, but it's different. At the beginning, we were going through a real grieving process, which tends to reduce somewhat I suppose, but to a lesser degree I still have that grieving experience.

64-year-old, Australian Uniting father,
bereaved 3 years

SUMMARY OF VISITATION EMOTIONS

Two major groups, or primary emotions, and six other specific emotions have been identified among cemetery visitors of diverse social and cultural backgrounds. The primary cemetery visitation emotions are identified as sorrow and solace.

As a group of emotions, sorrow includes grief and sadness, with the latter being the most frequently expressed specific emotion. The second major group of emotions is that of solace, including relief and peace. Other expressed bereavement emotions include guilt, respect, loss, loneliness, fear, and anger.

With the notable exception of the solace group (including relief and peace), all other emotions expressed by cemetery visitors have been previously recognized as common emotions of grief [4, 6-9]. However, the emotional benefits of cemetery visitation, which were reported by over 78% of visiting mourners in the Bereavement Study, have until now remained unrecognized by others.

Sorrow (including grief and sadness), and guilt, loss, loneliness, and anger were found to progressively subside in almost all regular visitors. This subsidence in intensity of emotions generally occurs rapidly from the funeral, or following a specific turning point, and commonly corresponds to abatement of cemetery visitation.

Through regular visitation soon after a loss, for most people, the cemetery progressively transforms from a "burial" place to a "healing" place.

Retention of the emotions of grief and sadness, guilt, loss, loneliness, and anger appears more common among those who avoid cemetery visitation, particularly during the early stages of bereavement. Deliberate avoidance of the cemetery may be indicative of a failure to embrace a satisfactory concept of personal grief-work, and may further deny these mourners the emotional benefits of cemetery visitation, which are evidently available to more regular visitors.

This concludes our review of cemetery visitation emotions. The next chapter considers visitors' comments on the frequency of their visits, and how this relates to the quantitative findings on visitation frequency.

REFERENCES

1. W. Weiten, *Psychology: Themes and variations* (4th ed.), Brooks/Cole, Pacific Grove, California, 1998.
2. R. Plutchik, Emotions and their vicissitudes: Emotions and psychopathology, in *Handbook of emotions,* M. Lewis and J. M. Haviland (eds.), Guilford Press, New York, 1993.
3. P. Bachelor, *Cemetery visitation: The place of the cemetery in the grief process,* unpublished Ph.D. thesis, Charles Sturt University, Wagga Wagga, 2001.
4. T. Attig, *How we grieve: Relearning the world,* Oxford University Press, New York, 1996.

5. S. R. Shuchter and S. Zisook, The course of normal grief, in *Handbook of bereavement: Theory, research, and intervention*, M. S. Stroebe, W. Stroebe, and R. O. Hansson (eds.), Cambridge University Press, Cambridge, 1993.

6. B. Raphael, *The anatomy of bereavement: A handbook for the caring professions*, Routledge, London, 1984.

7. C. M. Sanders, *Grief: The mourning after, dealing with adult bereavement*, Wiley Interscience, New York, 1989.

8. J. W. Worden, Grief counselling and grief therapy: A handbook for the mental health practitioner (2nd ed.), Routledge, London, 1991.

9. T. A. Rando, *Treatment of complicated mourning*, Research Press, Champaign, Illinois, 1993.

CHAPTER 11

Frequency

Frequencies of cemetery visits, and a general visitation trajectory, were clearly identified in the quantitative Visitation Study, and differences in frequencies of visitation were most evident by the service type, family religion, and the relationship of the decedent [1].

In this chapter, when and how changes in frequencies of visits occur, and the effects of specific turning points in the lives of visitors, are drawn from personal reflections of mourners in the Bereavement Study [2].

MODULATION

Almost two-thirds of visitors in the study recognized that a specific modulation of the frequency of their cemetery visits had occurred within a few years of the respective death.

Several mourners reported abatement in the frequency of visits occurring within weeks of the death and funeral. These reports were mostly from bereaved spouses who were quite free to visit as frequently as they felt any need or desire.

> I'd have been going there at least twice a week—sometimes three times a week—for the first six to eight weeks and then it rapidly tailed off.
>
> *62-year-old, Australian non-religious*
> *husband, bereaved 4½ years*

Some others reported abatement in the frequency of their visits occurring within months of the death and funeral.

> Straight after the funeral, I probably visited close to once a week—or at least every two weeks—then after a month or two, it dropped off to once a month. Now, I just go on the anniversary, birthday and spur of the moment visits.
>
> *40-year-old, Italian Catholic son,*
> *bereaved 3 years*

For the first six months after he passed away, I would go every Sunday, and after that—you know—not so much. I don't need to go so much.

66-year-old, Italian Catholic wife,
bereaved 5 years

And a small proportion of visitors reported abatement in the frequency of their visits occurring a year or more after the death and funeral.

For the first twelve months after he died, I came to the cemetery everyday. Now, it's every second day, or sometimes every third day.

33-year-old, Australian Catholic mother,
bereaved 2 years

For the first eighteen months, I used to go once a month, but it's gone to about once every three months now. . . . It changes; it's just something that happens progressively.

45-year-old, Australian non-religious female
secret-lover, bereaved 3 years

Others reported abatement in the frequency of their visits, without specifying how long after the death and funeral this had occurred. One of these mourners explained her personal feelings toward her own modulation of visitation frequency.

I used to go to the cemetery . . . everyday, or every second day. . . . I now visit perhaps every six weeks or so . . . not for the lack of love for him, it's just that you've got to get on with your life. The personal need to be there is not as great.

60-year-old, Australian non-religious
grandmother, bereaved 5 years

Interviews for the study occurred no greater than five years and no less than two months after the death of someone significant; and just over a third of visiting mourners reported no modulation of frequency of their visits having yet occurred since bereavement. Sustained visitation may relate to fulfilling a sense of obligation, or to an acquired habit.

I visit Mum and Dad's grave every Monday, Wednesday, Friday and on the weekend—every week. I used to go three times with Dad, to visit Mum, and I just kept the tradition going; that's continued through.

47-year-old, Australian daughter of no specific
faith, bereaved 5 months

Every day I go, ever since she passed away, except . . . when I went to Malta, otherwise every day I go.

66-year-old, Maltese Catholic husband,
bereaved 4½ years

One young mother found it difficult to imagine that her then very-frequent visitation was likely to modulate at all.

So many people say, "As time goes on, you won't feel the need to go there as often"; and I know older parts of the cemetery get visited less. But at this stage, I find that hard to imagine. I can't really see what time is going to do in this sense to me. I can't see how that will change.

27-year-old, Australian Catholic mother,
bereaved 10 months

But many other visitors found that a progressive distancing from their loss seemed to occur naturally with the passing of time.

I think the change is just part of the grieving process. You feel that you need to go because your hurt is still there, but as you start to get your life back together, or back to normality, the pain eases off. I think it's just a natural thing.

40-year-old, Italian Catholic son,
bereaved 3 years

Time is a healer.

62-year-old, Australian non-religious grandfather,
bereaved 5 years

TURNING POINTS

Some visitors recognized specific changes in the frequencies of their visits, corresponding to decisive turning points in the course of their grief, or to other personal circumstances. Such turning points may evidently be intellectual or emotional.

I'd have been going there at least twice a week—sometimes three times a week—for the first six to eight weeks, and then it rapidly tailed off. I'd go back and I'd start thinking, "I'm not doing myself or anybody any good here"—but I still missed her. . . . The space has become greater as realism, logic and objectivity all begin to play a much larger part.

62-year-old, Australian non-religious
husband, bereaved 4½ years

I feel I have less of a need to visit now than I did earlier, but I'll still go. It won't be as often as it was in the first two-and-a-half to three years, but I will always go.

35-year-old, Australian non-religious
granddaughter, bereaved 4 years

For some, professional guidance may provide an emotionally-positive turning point.

I found one of the best things that helped me, was . . . the funeral director's Christmas seminar, a year after he died. It was the best thing I'd done. Those experts put me on track, because I really thought that I was going mental—but I wasn't of course. Then I started to think, the next time someone asks me,

"How are you going?" I'm going to say, "Fantastic!" And that was my turning point; it honestly was.

60-year-old, Australian non-religious
grandmother, bereaved 5 years

And a return to routine commitments, including work, can also present a turning point in visitation by replacing one's ability to visit very frequently.

Straight after Mum's funeral I went on a daily basis, because I had about two-and-a-half weeks off from work, but since I've been back, it's just on weekends.

27-year-old, Greek Orthodox daughter,
bereaved 4 months

SUMMARY OF VISITATION FREQUENCY

Self-reported abatement of frequency of cemetery visits was found to be consistent with the Visitation Study's quantitative findings of a visitation trajectory (Figure 5.5, p. 55 [2]). Most visitors reported the frequency of their visits to have recognizably abated, and this abatement was most evident within weeks or months of the death and funeral, but in some cases, occurred a year or more later.

Most mourners found that abatement of their cemetery visitation correlated to subsidence in the intensity of their grief emotions, suggesting that cemetery visitation is commonly an important element of personal grief management.

Customary pre-bereavement practices of seeing a loved one and giving gifts on personal and public anniversaries and religious festivals are commonly substituted after death with visiting the grave or memorial and placing flowers, greeting cards, and other symbolic gifts. Such substitute symbolic giving manifests ongoing love toward maintaining the relationship, and mitigates the emotions of loss, particularly at times of specific personal remembrance.

For most mourners, the cemetery provides an essential place of focus, and for some it is the only place where vital communication with the decedent may occur on such important occasions.

Cemetery visitation is a crucial aspect of working through grief for many mourners. It allows the full emotions of grief to be mitigated through keeping a part of the decedent alive within the life of the mourner. And it is evidently of most value in the early stages of bereavement, as this value usually diminishes progressively.

This concludes the personal reflections of mourners on how changes in frequencies of visits occur and the effects of specific turning points in their lives. The next chapter acknowledges that not all mourners visit a cemetery and identifies common reasons why this is so.

REFERENCES

1. P. Bachelor, *Cemetery visitors in Australia,* Eleventh National Conference of the Australian Cemeteries & Crematoria Association, Alice Springs, August 30-September 3, 1998.
2. P. Bachelor, *Cemetery visitation: The place of the cemetery in the grief process,* unpublished Ph.D. thesis, Charles Sturt University, Wagga Wagga, 2001.

CHAPTER 12

Non-Visitation Reasons

Previous chapters have focused on common reasons for visiting cemeteries, frequency of visitation, common associated activities and emotions. This chapter now acknowledges that not all bereaved people necessarily visit any cemetery.

Of 27 informants in the Bereavement Study, four were not cemetery visitors at all; and 10 others, who generally were, commented on either their own reasons for non-visitation at various times, or the non-visitation of others. Common reasons for some mourners not visiting cemeteries were found to include: non-interment of remains, inability to access the cemetery, grief repression and avoidance, religious restrictions, and no perception of any need to visit [1]. Mourners' own understandings of these reasons are now presented.

NON-INTERMENT OF REMAINS

Many families that choose cremation have no specific reason to visit a cemetery. Recent Australian data indicates the specific interment and memorialization rate of cremated remains within cemeteries to be only 42%, and a further 7% are strewn within cemetery grounds [2].

Alternate destinations of cremated remains include scattering elsewhere in accord with cultural traditions, in favorite places in accord with modern rites, and temporary storage at private residences and funeral parlors with no commitment to any ultimate placement.

In at least some cases of non-interment, fulfilling a perceived desire of the decedent becomes a more important factor than facilitating grief resolution of the survivors.

> Both my mother and father were cremated, and there are no ashes, no plots: nothing. That's what they wanted; that's what they got.
>
> *62-year-old, Australian non-religious*
> *grandfather, bereaved 5 years*

Other common reasons for not interring remains at a cemetery include withholding them from others due to family disputes or unresolved personal issues, and indecision by principle mourners or those with a right of say.

INABILITY TO ACCESS THE CEMETERY

Several mourners in the study identified proximity of the cemetery as a significant factor in the frequency of their visits, and in some cases their ability to visit at all. Factors inhibiting access include mobility of the mourner, lack of personal transport or satisfactory public transport, and remote location of the cemetery, including interstate and overseas sites, as families continue to be more widely scattered than in previous generations.

GRIEF REPRESSION

By deliberately avoiding the cemetery, and thereby seeking to avoid confronting the reality it presents, some mourners strive to bury distressing thoughts and feelings into their sub-consciousness.

One widow in the study not only refused to attend her husband's funeral, but also to visit his grave since.

> I feel that if I went to that cemetery, I'd feel that it just happened yesterday. I would feel that I'd lost him all over again and I'd start from the beginning now. It makes it definite, you know. But perhaps I'm playing a game where I think he's away somewhere and perhaps he'll come back. I don't want to look at that ground and know he's there—it's too final: it's absolutely too final. I keep away from there.
>
> *75-year-old, Australian Catholic wife,*
> *bereaved 14 months*

Other mourners also consider it preferable to repress unpleasant memories, and to avoid potentially recurrent grief reactions to visiting, by staying away from the cemetery.

> Why put yourself through another sadness when you don't need to? I know that if I went there, all these memories from the accident would all come back; so it's best, I think.
>
> *43-year-old, Australian sister-in-law of*
> *eclectic faith, bereaved 3 years*

> Our younger daughter doesn't like to go at all. She'll go if we want her to come with us, but she doesn't really like it and won't go on her own.
>
> *64-year-old, Australian Uniting mother,*
> *bereaved 3 years*

RELIGIOUS RESTRICTIONS

Cemetery visitation may be regulated by specific religious observances of some faiths, for example Judaism, where:

> After a funeral, the immediate family is not permitted to go to the cemetery for thirty days, or four weeks.
>
> *37-year-old, Australian Jewish sister,*
> *bereaved 8 months*

But as well as refraining from visiting during certain periods and set holy days, adherents of some faiths may, on the other hand, also be expected to visit and pay respects on other specific occasions.

NO PERCEIVED NEED TO VISIT

Some bereaved individuals, particularly those who may have been less emotionally dependent on their relationship with the decedent, simply do not experience any perception of need to visit the cemetery.

> Personally, I don't need to go.
> *25-year-old, Australian Catholic grandson, bereaved 1 year*

No perception of a need to visit relates to an absence of any of the reasons for visitation experienced by other mourners. The major reasons are to fulfill a sense of obligation, to maintain a significant emotional bond, and to seek solace from the emotions of grief.

SUMMARY OF NON-VISITATION REASONS

Toward understanding the place of the cemetery within contexts of grief, it is essential to recognize that not all mourners visit a cemetery. Visitation may not occur if the remains are not interred in a cemetery, or if the mourner is unable to travel to the cemetery, represses their grief, is subject to religious restrictions, or simply feels no need to visit.

While the cemetery facilitates vital opportunities for many mourners to work through their grief, others endeavor to manage without any opportunity or perceived need to visit.

Visiting the location of the remains of a decedent is less important to mourners who hold little or no perception of association between the body and spirit of the deceased. To these mourners, little sense of obligation to visit exists, nor does any desire to communicate with the decedent, and solace is therefore less likely to be attainable from carrying out such activities. Those who may be genuinely unable to travel to the cemetery, or whose visitation may be restricted by religious observance, would also be free of any sense of such obligation.

In his study of London widows, Parkes found that those who initially repressed grief, showed little or no emotional response or formal mourning, and avoided visiting the grave or crematorium, were found to ultimately suffer more psychological and physical problems than those whom he reports "broke down" in the first week. Parkes also found that those who "held back" became more psychologically disturbed around the anniversary of death [3].

Osterweis, Solomon, and Green conclude that mourners likely to become stuck in pathological grief reactions are those whose pre-bereavement response patterns were to avoid confrontation and to escape from difficult situations [4]. An implication of this is that those inclined to avoid cemetery visitation, specifically to evade acceptance of the fact of death, or to evade sadness or recurrent grief, may be more likely to suffer pathological outcomes in the long-run. In the recent Bereavement Study, some participants who had deliberately avoided visiting the cemetery to evade its confrontation had subsequently been clinically diagnosed as suffering pathological grief.

Self-justification for not visiting the cemetery appears to be an important factor in averting feelings of guilt at not meeting what is otherwise a commonly perceived sense of obligation. But deliberate avoidance of cemetery visitation in the absence of self-justification appears indicative of unresolved and potentially pathological grief.

The main reasons for cemetery visitation incorporate expression of grief, while grief repression is a major factor in much non-visitation. Since satisfactory expression of grief is commonly recognized as being essential toward a satisfactory bereavement outcome for most mourners, and repression of grief is associated with incubating pathological conditions [3-9] cemetery visitation is evidently a highly important component of grief management for most mourners in Western societies.

Typical patterns of cemetery visitation behavior are indicative of healthy bereavement outcome; while abnormal behaviors, including the extremes of avoidance and chronic daily visitation indicate significant unresolved issues.

Sadly, many mourners denied a meaningful locus for the expression of their grief, as often occurs through the scattering or non-interment of cremated remains, may be expected to retain unresolved grief issues indefinitely.

This concludes our discussion of evident common reasons why some mourners do not visit a cemetery. Common reasons for not visiting were found to include non-interment of remains, inability to access the cemetery, grief repression, religious restrictions, and no perception of any need to visit.

The following chapter will consider personal values of funerals, cemeteries, memorials, and grave or memorial visitation to mourners of various social and cultural backgrounds.

REFERENCES

1. P. Bachelor, *Cemetery visitation: The place of the cemetery in the grief process,* unpublished Ph.D. thesis, Charles Sturt University, Wagga Wagga, 2001.
2. Australian Cemeteries & Crematoria Association, Cremation in Australia, *ACCA News,* pp. 9-11, Autumn 1998.
3. C. M. Parkes, *Bereavement: Studies of grief in adult life* (3rd ed.), Penguin, London, 1996.
4. M. Osterweis, F. Solomon, and M. Green (eds.), *Bereavement: Reactions, consequences, and care,* National Academy Press, Washington, D.C., 1984.
5. B. Raphael, *The anatomy of bereavement: A handbook for the caring professions,* Routledge, London, 1984.
6. C. M. Sanders, *Grief: The mourning after, dealing with adult bereavement,* Wiley Interscience, New York, 1989.
7. J. W. Worden, *Grief counselling and grief therapy: A handbook for the mental health practitioner* (2nd ed.), Routledge, London, 1991.
8. T. A. Rando, *Treatment of complicated mourning,* Research Press, Champaign, Illinois, 1993.
9. M. S. Stroebe, W. Stroebe, and R. O. Hansson (eds.), *Handbook of bereavement: Theory, research, and intervention,* Cambridge University Press, Cambridge, 1993.

CHAPTER 13

Personal Values

Part C has so far considered various aspects of cemetery visitation, with the preceding chapter specifically reviewing common reasons for non-visitation. In this chapter, we now explore personal values of the funeral, cemetery, memorial, and grave or memorial visitation, from the perspectives of mourners of various social and cultural backgrounds.

The most common values of cemeteries to mourners will be seen to include sacredness, cultural values, social support, heritage, and remembrance.

THE FUNERAL

The funeral is the rite through which mourners physically and symbolically enter the cemetery. The Visitation Study identified funeral participants to account for 23% of all cemetery visits, with many of these people attending the cemetery for their first time [1]. But other than being commonly considered an essential customary ritual, or perhaps a religious obligation in the disposition of the remains of a decedent, personal values of a funeral are not well recognized.

There are evidently several reasons for holding funerals, and the personal values of funerals vary considerably. Funerals are seen to have traditionally represented a means of honoring the dead, of mitigating the impact of death on survivors, of re-affirming family and community ties, and of re-stating religious beliefs [2].

But as Walter recognizes, specific values of funerals vary greatly, and expressed meanings depend on just who is asked.

> Clergy and undertakers tell me that, "Funerals are for the living," and that, "The funeral's purpose is to help the grief process." But ask people why they attended a particular funeral and they reply, "in order to pay my last respects"; in other words, they have come for the sake of the deceased. Or they may say they have come to support the next of kin. Ask next of kin and they are likely

to say that it's an ordeal they have to go through for the sake of everyone else, because holding a funeral is the done thing. Hindus will say they are there to release the soul of the deceased, traditional Catholics that they are there to say a mass for the deceased. Apart from some members of the "expressive" caring professions, no attenders say they are there to help their own grief process. It is a matter of religion, of the socially done thing and ultimately of human decency [3, p. 156].

Walter further reports agreement at a workshop on funerals in London, that the deceased person should take center stage and the funeral should reflect his or her unique life rather than the commercial, bureaucratic, or religious interests of functionaries. He considers that even if using religious language, the funeral should be what the Australians call "life-centered," adding that in Britain, explicitly humanist funerals which self-consciously set out to celebrate a life are still rare, but increasing [3].

On the general values of a funeral, he concludes that:

To attend a funeral is ultimately about neither therapy nor psychology. It is a statement of the humanity of the one who has died. And that is why people continue to go to funerals, why funerals cannot be defined in terms of whatever therapeutic function they may or may not have for the grieving, and why therapy and the funeral can never be reduced one to the other [3, p. 180].

Viewing the body prior to or during a funeral can reassure mourners that the decedent is at peace, provide a personal opportunity to say goodbye, and allay otherwise possible concerns about the correct content of the coffin. In the Bereavement Study, half of the informants had attended a viewing and without exception considered it to have been a positive experience [4]. Typical comments included the following.

I didn't actually see Dad when he died, but I saw him at the funeral parlor. It was terrific to see him then, dressed up and ready for his next adventure. We put his fishing rod in with him, and it was good to see him. To view the body was good.

40-year-old, Italian Catholic son, bereaved 3 years

The viewing was good, because only a couple of days before, we saw her being sick and all that. She didn't look very nice then; she'd lost heaps and heaps of weight and she looked like a skeleton. It was just good to see her virtually looking well—because she did. They did a really good job; they had even done her nails. She looked like a big china doll, and she was buried in her wedding dress.

51-year-old, Australian non-religious husband, bereaved 2 months

Mum asked us if we wanted to have a viewing and the consensus was: "Yes." So we all went to the funeral parlor together, and I must say I found that rather strange. I didn't quite know what to expect, but I'm glad I did it. I was really pleased with the way she looked. She looked really well actually, considering that she was rather ill and a tired old lady when she died. I think they did a really good job, and we picked out the clothes and what-have-you.

35-year-old, Australian non-religious
granddaughter, bereaved 4 years

People had told me that to see someone when they have died helps you accept death a lot better, so I saw him and it was just like he was asleep. And I think that really helped me, because I didn't really feel that he had died—that he'd been in a lot of pain or anything—because he looked really peaceful; he just looked like he was asleep.

45-year-old, Australian non-religious female
secret-lover, bereaved 3 years

The presence of other relatives, friends and associates at a funeral can be very important to principle mourners, who may measure the success of the funeral, the community respect and significance of the decedent, and the extent to which their grief is shared and they are cared about, by the number of attendees at the funeral.

I think I drew more solace from the number of people who came to the funeral; it was quite an enormous turnout. Many came because of the military association with myself, but a huge amount were people whom [my wife] had somehow touched in her lifetime, even back to people she went to school with.

62-year-old, Australian non-religious
husband, bereaved 4½ years

The service was a great tribute to [my daughter], that so many people attended from old to quite young. A number of children that she'd taught came along, and I thought that was a wonderful tribute. There was perhaps about 350 people there in all, and everything went very well.

64-year-old, Australian Uniting father,
bereaved 3 years

The Italian way is that people come and visit you at the home prior to the actual funeral and give their condolences personally. The number of people that filtered in through those three days was unbelievable. That is just the Italian way, I suppose. It's just amazing to see how many people are actually prepared to do that. But then, they also come to the funeral. The numbers and just the support—it's just incredible. People you wouldn't expect just turn up, and it makes you feel that you do mean something to other people, and that's good.

40-year-old, Italian Catholic son,
bereaved 3 years

All the time I remember the funeral. He had a good funeral—good people came. The church was full: yeah, it was full. There were his mates from work and my relatives and my friends. He had a good funeral.

66-year-old, Italian Catholic wife,
bereaved 5 years

However, with a particularly large turnout, principal mourners may feel some loss of control over the event. The intimately bereaved may not want to publicly share their loss, and so may feel deprived if they consider that the general focus of the funeral is somehow directed away from their intense personal grief.

> There was a great turnout: 900-odd people. We asked for a private burial. I would've liked it even a little bit more private than it was; but my husband's family are Italian and they take "immediate family" to include cousins and second cousins and third cousins. We just had close friends and family at the burial, and I'm really glad. I still wish it was smaller, but it was fine at the time.
>
> *27-year-old, Australian Catholic mother,*
> *bereaved 10 months*

The funeral can also present an opportunity to reconcile differences, and to conclude physical relationships through bidding the decedent a final goodbye.

> Through the funeral, I definitely had a good opportunity to say my personal goodbye.
>
> *70-year-old, Italian Catholic wife, bereaved 3 years*

> I was very happy with the opportunity to see him at the funeral home. I feel that gave me a good opportunity to say goodbye to him.
>
> *45-year-old, Australian non-religious female*
> *secret-lover, bereaved 3 years*

> The church was packed, because she was a very lovable woman. I think the funeral is how people come together—you know—saying goodbye. Yeah; I think it's more saying goodbye.
>
> *66-year-old, Maltese Catholic husband,*
> *bereaved 4½ years*

But with some traumatic losses, personal reconciliation may not be considered possible, and funerals do not always provide the same opportunities to all mourners.

> I know that a lot of people see the funeral as a time to say goodbye, but for me it wasn't; it wasn't a goodbye. It's not the way I look at it, in any way.
>
> *37-year-old, Australian Jewish sister,*
> *bereaved 8 months*

And funeral rituals need not be traditional. They may be of very modern origin, and even specifically invented to express certain characteristics of the decedent. Personalizing the funeral is very important to many mourners.

> We chose little bits of music that [my grandson] loved. We all clapped our hands together and that helped us more. There was a tape recording of his favorite little piece of music that he used to jump around with. All the family there had to jump around and clap our hands and we'd all fall down.
>
> *60-year-old, Australian non-religious*
> *grandmother, bereaved 5 years*

I think the funeral and the way things went was really helpful at the time, because it's something to work to. I sat down and wrote out the service and typed it out. It's important that you put into it what you want to go into it and don't leave it to other people to do, because I think you'd be sorry later.

64-year-old, Australian Uniting mother, bereaved 3 years

He was cremated and it was—it sounds very strange—but it was the best funeral that I've ever been to. They had singing; they had funny stories; they had lots of people. Yes it was a really big funeral and really good. To me it wasn't a sad day. It was a celebration of his life and what he'd meant to a lot of people. It was different.

45-year-old, Australian non-religious female
secret-lover, bereaved 3 years

It was probably one of the most moving and best funerals I've ever been to. It was at home in exactly the same place we were married. The flag was at half-mast and the cows were in the front paddock. Then we drove to town to the cemetery. There we had a graveside service and . . . then she had a five-airplane fly-by. That was just magic because she was very active in the aero club; she made that club.

51-year-old, Australian non-religious
husband, bereaved 2 months

My second-eldest brother did the service; he's a minister. One of his sons played the saxophone and the other son played the piano. They played "Amazing Grace" and because that was [my brother-in-law's] favorite song it was extremely emotional. And my Mum got up and read; so a lot of the family actually took part.

43-year-old, Australian eclectic
sister-in-law, bereaved 3 years

[My daughter's] funeral was very important to me. We had a family friend that's a priest, who understands all my views and opinions; he did our wedding and my brother's funeral. I wanted some certain things done in the service. I wanted the priest to stand up there and yell at God for me; that was really important to me.

27-year-old, Australian Catholic mother, bereaved 10 months

The funeral can also present opportunities to construct a fuller personality for one whose life may have been all too brief, and to impress on others the significance of one whom they may not have come to know.

The funeral was very, very important—very important. And I wanted it to be really, really sad. I wanted everyone to be howling, because they should be, because it's my little baby. A lot of those people had never met her, so it was important that everyone walked away feeling like they'd known her; that's why we had a fairly lengthy type of eulogy. Even though she was only seven months, we tried to make it like everyone could share part of her life: that was very important.

27-year-old, Australian Catholic mother, bereaved 10 months

We wanted pictures of her in the entrance there, so I guess we made it really hard for people. We wanted people to know that she was there, and we made sure that they did know. And I think that's been good ever since, because people have this picture of our little girl. The day itself was really important to me. I'm very much a pragmatist. I knew she was dead. I knew she was dead before the funeral; it wasn't as though I needed the funeral to tell me she was dead. I needed the funeral for other people to know that she had been alive. That's what I needed the funeral for; and that's what it did, I think.

> *37-year-old, Australian Baptist father,*
> *bereaved 3 years*

The rite of the funeral may also be seen as the completion of immediate practicalities, and the commencement of formally working through grief. To many mourners, this marks the beginning of a gradual process of returning to some sense of normality.

Maybe when somebody passes away then a process has to begin. I think it's something that you dread, so once it's over you're relieved when that part of the process is done; it's something you don't have to talk about or worry about any more. I think the only thing the funeral did for me was let me say, "Well it's done; it's done now." It is a definite finalization.

> *37-year-old, Australian Jewish sister,*
> *bereaved 8 months*

I think the funeral is very helpful. It helps you come to terms with it, because it's like final. It sort of ends the whole process from the time of death to the burial, and then you can sort of get back to your normal way of life. Obviously weeks, months, or a year goes by while you get back to normal, but at least it's a starting point.

> *40-year-old, Italian Catholic son,*
> *bereaved 3 years*

But not everyone who is recently bereaved necessarily recognizes any specific personal value from a funeral.

I think it was just a relief that Dad moved on. I think that's how it was with the whole family, you know. One brother didn't even turn up. . . . There wasn't one tear. Most people who went there, in my mind, were just making sure that he was going down, you know. I went along because, you know, it was the thing to do.

> *54-year-old Australian Catholic son,*
> *bereaved 10 months*

I'm not a funeral person. It was just a hell of a day finishing off a hell of a week, and nothing could have made it better or worse.

> *62-year-old, Australian non-religious*
> *grandfather, bereaved 5 years*

To some mourners, the funeral is regarded as a choice-less though necessary imposition.

I just never expected it to happen. The funeral was another part that I suppose we had to get through; we didn't have a choice. I mean, what could you do with him otherwise? If there was another alternative, I'm sure I would've considered it. But I knew that's what happens when someone dies; you have to bury them, and I had to accept it. There was no choice about it.

33-year-old, Australian Catholic mother,
bereaved 2 years

It was totally emotional. We just did not want—if at all possible—to be in that situation.

37-year-old, Australian Jewish sister,
bereaved 8 months

And, to those seeking to avoid preconceived unpleasant experiences, and who perhaps sub-consciously strive to repress hurtful memories, the funeral may be considered an affront to evade.

I wasn't going to sit there in front of a box and know that he was in it. My two daughters planned the funeral; I had nothing whatsoever to do with it. . . . I could listen to the tape of the service, without even crying; but it doesn't at all make me wish that I had gone to the funeral—no way—never! No, I couldn't. It'd be the last memory, you know—a box with his body in it—no way!

75-year-old, Australian Catholic wife,
bereaved 14 months

But to many mourners, the funeral presents a crucial opportunity for the ultimate expression of their love.

The funeral ritual gives you a feeling that you have done whatever is required on behalf of the deceased, that you have transferred merit. You feel that the funeral gives the satisfaction of having done everything possible for the deceased.

59-year-old, Sri Lankan Buddhist daughter,
bereaved 3 months

The funeral was something that had to be done, but it was also our final respect to her. It was the last time that we could actually show how much we loved her. To me, it was the last thing I could actually do for Mum, so of course you try and do everything to perfection.

27-year-old, Greek Orthodox daughter,
bereaved 4 months

THE CEMETERY

The study also identified expressed personal values of cemeteries to those who are recently bereaved. A cemetery value is here defined as any significance or importance of the cemetery to a bereaved person.

The personal values identified include sacredness, cultural values, social support, heritage, and remembrance. The following sections present participants' own comments on these specific values.

Sacredness

Various religions, churches, denominations, and sects tend to revere cemeteries as sacred, and often consecrate specifically dedicated cemeteries or respective compartments within public cemeteries.

Some Catholics specifically mentioned that they considered the cemetery to hold a similar degree of sacredness as a church.

> It is a sacred, holy place, like the church is.
>
> *70-year-old, Italian Catholic wife,*
> *bereaved 3 years*

While other mourners of various faiths also consider the cemetery to be sacred, but not to the same degree as a church, temple, synagogue, or mosque.

> I believe the cemetery is a sacred place, but I'm not sure how to explain it. I think on a personal basis, that it's not as holy as the church. It has that holiness in it, but it's not as holy as the church, you know.
>
> *27-year-old, Greek Orthodox daughter,*
> *bereaved 4 months*

And others consider that the cemetery should certainly be venerated, but for non-religious reasons.

> I see the cemetery as being sacred to the memory of the people who are there, rather than sacred in the Catholic sense.
>
> *62-year-old, Australian non-religious*
> *husband, bereaved 4½ years*

However, several mourners of various religious perspectives specifically mentioned that to them the cemetery has no specific sense of sacredness.

> To me, the cemetery is not sacred—as in holy, like the synagogue—but I respect it.
>
> *37-year-old, Australian Jewish sister,*
> *bereaved 8 months*

> To me, the cemetery doesn't have any sacredness . . . or much other significance.
>
> *37-year-old, Australian Baptist father,*
> *bereaved 3 years*

Cultural Values

Several mourners expressed their opinions of the cultural values of the cemetery, with some commenting on various opportunities that the cemetery provides for the continuation of various cultural traditions.

> I think it is traditional—when you visit a gravesite—in Jewish religion, to put a pebble on the grave as a mark of respect and to mark the fact that you've been.
>
> *37-year-old, Australian Jewish sister,*
> *bereaved 8 months*

> The mausoleum is . . . how they do it overseas. So for the people here who immigrated, it's just back to what they were used to; it's their traditional way of burying people.
>
> *40-year-old, Italian Catholic son,*
> *bereaved 3 years*

But cultural traditions, and the value of such traditions, can also vary by the specific geographic origins of mourners.

> I understand that certain Orthodox cultures have feast days on weekends, and they take their food and eat it with the person that has passed away. . . . I think it depends on which part of Greece you come from.
>
> *27-year-old, Greek Orthodox daughter,*
> *bereaved 4 months*

And cultural traditions remain subject to modernization and changing values.

> Some Buddhists are buried and some are cremated. . . . In our area, the customs are different from other areas. . . . Younger people tend to be buried and older people tend to be cremated in accordance with customary traditions, but not everywhere.
>
> *59-year-old, Sri Lankan Buddhist daughter,*
> *bereaved 3 months*

Western cemeteries generally embraced concepts of multiculturalism and non-discrimination during the 1980s; with the effect that compartmentalization by religion is no longer practiced in most contemporary general cemetery developments. But, while non-denominational (or multi-denominational) compartments may appeal to the socially-concerned, but inexperienced or uninvolved observer, this relatively new practice offends the traditions of many religious groups and cemetery stakeholders who clearly favor such discrimination.

In some places, Jewish groups in particular have enjoyed recent success in lobbying governments for their own exclusive cemeteries. So unless general cemeteries do cater well for the specific needs of their various clients, including Jews, Muslims, Roman Catholics, Eastern Orthodox, Buddhists, Hindus, and Taoists, as well as Protestants and those of no faith, then a growing demand may be expected for diverse, exclusive, ethnic cemeteries.

Some mourners in the study specifically referred to the importance of exclusive cemeteries or dedicated compartments within general cemeteries.

> I would like to go in the Orthodox area, because of my religion . . . of course the Orthodoxy does play an enormous role. I'd feel comfortable in the fact that I'm amongst others of the same religion. It's the place to be. . . . Of course, once we go it doesn't really matter where our body is—it's our soul that plays the important role—but you still want to be amongst those who have had the same beliefs as yourself.
>
> *27-year-old, Greek Orthodox daughter,*
> *bereaved 4 months*

> Judaism was really important to him. . . . So I think if he had a choice, he would be very happy that he was buried as a Jew.
>
> *37-year-old, Australian Jewish sister,*
> *bereaved 8 months*

Social Support

Several mourners commented on varying degrees of social support either given or received within the cemetery, and each considered this type of support to be beneficial toward overcoming grief. Through the sharing of experiences and offering mutual support, self-help groups develop naturally within larger cemeteries and operate among regular visitors.

Groups of young mothers were found to coordinate their visits to specific children's areas, to cooperatively maintain each other's graves, and to support each other through reciprocative counseling. Other mutual support activities were reported among visitors to specific cemetery sections catering to Italian-Catholic, Greek-Orthodox, and Muslim families.

These naturally constructed self-help groups evidently comprise mourners who may have experienced a similar type of loss, or are of similar ethnicity, including their first language and religious faith.

Within the study, most of these specific mourners recognized mutual benefits from two-way sharing with other cemetery visitors.

> In talking to other mums that have lost kids, we've developed a great bond, because we're all going through the same thing. In some ways, it's more helpful than talking to a counselor who's gone through textbooks, but hasn't gone through our emotions and how hard it is. So yes, a lot of us mums have become quite close.
>
> *33-year-old, Australian Catholic mother,*
> *bereaved 2 years*

And some found their own tragedies easier to bear after speaking with other visitors who had evidently suffered what they then considered to be even greater losses.

You know, once we stop and talk to people, we find there are two boys and one was sick and one had an accident; they're both buried in the same grave: brothers . . . the same day . . . One is twenty-five and one is twenty-two. So when we see that, I say, "Gee; we lost one and they've lost two."

The poor boy we talked to yesterday . . . his sisters died. . . . His father is an ambulance man and . . . they rang his father and said: "There's an accident." And he was with his ambulance and he . . . said, "Oh, gee; my two daughters and they both are twins." So when we learn these, you know, we are getting a little bit of relief. We're saying we are worse, but some people are more worse, you know.

52-year-old, Turkish Muslim father,
bereaved 14 months

However, sometimes, social contact within the cemetery may be considered to be beneficial to just one of the parties.

I've met . . . a family that has lost a son, just across from Dad. They're there often and I think it helps them—not me—but it probably helps them for me to talk to them.

40-year-old, Italian Catholic son,
bereaved 3 years

Social support may also include professional counseling, and one mourner commented on the personal benefit she derived from practical counseling within the cemetery.

I've been seeing a counselor; he's helped me a real lot, you know. . . . We'd have a walk around the cemetery and he'd come to my parents' grave, you know. It was good to sit down and talk.

47-year-old, Australian daughter of no specific
faith, bereaved 5 months

Several mourners specifically mentioned that they had formed close friendships with others they had met at the cemetery. One couple first met the parents of their son's best friend within the cemetery. In this case, both families had lost their sons through separate motorcycle accidents eight months apart.

Yeah, we met first at the cemetery and then we met at a restaurant. We are best family friends now; we visit each other and just talk, you know. We try to give us a bit of comfort, you know.

52-year-old, Turkish Muslim father,
bereaved 14 months

Several young mothers spoke of the values of relationships formed with empathetic peers befriended at the cemetery. In a number of cases, these new friends had become each other's most valuable social support, when even family and close friends failed to understand.

Some people . . . just fumble for words and yap on, trying to make you feel better. But usually what happens is I just say, "Yeah, yeah; no worries." Then I'll hang up and ring one of the other mums from the cemetery and say, "You wouldn't believe what this idiot just said to me." So we have big bitch sessions about all the silly things people say to us.

27-year-old, Australian Catholic mother,
bereaved 10 months

One couple reported that the mother, who spends at least two hours every day at their son's grave, actively seeks to establish relationships with new mourners "joining" the cemetery, and that she maintains a log of their personal details for her future reference.

As soon as she sees someone digging the grave she goes and talks to them and asks them. We just go in and meet each other and talk and she writes it in the book.

52-year-old, Turkish Muslim father,
bereaved 14 months

But other mourners spoke of reasons for avoiding social contacts within the cemetery. Even other family members may be deliberately avoided during early grief, so as not to encroach on each other's personal time and to minimize the emotional experience of visiting.

In the early days, we'd . . . always bump into one of the family. . . . We'd more-or-less like pass in the dark. It's not that we weren't talking to each other: we were. But we'd just say, "Hello," and they'd go their way and we'd go our way.

60-year-old, Australian non-religious
grandmother, bereaved 5 years

Some visiting mourners also endeavor to avoid specific others who may be less considerate of their needs, or who may be obsessive, imposing and distressing.

There's one woman there that I don't like to speak to as much. . . . She just focuses on her daughter's illness. When she sees me she wants to discuss what ward [my daughter] was in and what doctors she had and that sort of stuff. . . . and I find that she brings me down. I've actually turned around the car and gone to see someone else or gone to the canteen when I've seen her car.

27-year-old, Australian Catholic mother,
bereaved 10 months

Heritage

Several mourners in the study considered that the cemetery holds some heritage value. Perceptions of heritage include cultural heritage, local, and family histories.

One mourner considered that the heritage value of a specific religious cemetery is dependent upon its cultural exclusivity.

There are lots of people we know who are buried there; it definitely has heritage value. If there wasn't a Jewish cemetery, as such, and you were able to be buried anywhere, then I don't think it would have any heritage value.

37-year-old, Australian Jewish sister,
bereaved 8 months

Another considered that the cemetery's heritage value relates to its documented local history.

I suppose it would have some heritage value. It tells you a lot about the town, because you can usually see in a mining town that the people died a lot younger—mainly accidents—than in an agricultural town. You can learn a lot about a place by its cemetery; and they are interesting places.

51-year-old, Australian non-religious
husband, bereaved 2 months

To at least one young man, the cemetery's heritage value increases with progressive occupation by members of his family.

We're creating a family heritage at the cemetery. We've actually reserved a fairly large family plot—because of the size of the family—and everyone's got wishes where they want to be buried. . . . It definitely creates a heritage. It's got that name there for future generations to go back and look at. . . . I also find it very interesting in historical value.

25-year-old, Australian Catholic grandson,
bereaved 1 year

And a mature husband expressed his concern at the possible loss of heritage through the concept of grave renewal.

I am appalled that in a country as large as Australia, we think we can recycle gravesites. I can understand it in countries where land is at a premium, such as Japan and in parts of Europe, but we don't have that problem. The problem may come of having to put a cemetery somewhere where it may be difficult for people to get to, if you run out of space in suburbia—which we will do. Land is finite; but I think the loss of heritage is terrible.

62-year-old, Australian non-religious
husband, bereaved 4½ years

But just as many mourners commented that to them the cemetery had no heritage value, as did those specifically noting it to be significant in this respect. And some inferred that the respective cemetery's lack of heritage value related to their personal disconnection from ancestral burial.

This cemetery doesn't have any history to me. All my family is buried in England.

67-year-old, English Salvation Army wife,
bereaved 4 years

Remembrance

Several visiting mourners discussed remembrance values, and the majority of these people considered the opportunities that the cemetery presents for memorialization to be significant.

> One of the most important things about the cemetery is that there's somewhere for the memorial, to remember him by. He's got his place in the ground, or his place in the world, so to speak. His name is always going to be written down and not forgotten.
>
> *25-year-old, Australian Catholic grandson,*
> *bereaved 1 year*

Others spoke of the focus provided by the cemetery as a place to go and remember the decedent on specific occasions.

> You never, ever forget those that have gone, but I guess the cemetery gives you an opportunity to go and remember them on the special occasions, such as birthdays and the like.
>
> *64-year-old, Australian Uniting father,*
> *bereaved 3 years*

However, not all considered the cemetery to be necessarily essential in providing remembrance value.

> I don't think that you have to go to the cemetery to remember the person. . . . I mean, you remember what you remember yourself; you don't have to go and visit a cemetery.
>
> *45-year-old, Australian non-religious female*
> *secret-lover, bereaved 3 years*

Summary of Cemetery Values

That the cemetery is as sacred as a church to some mourners should not be surprising, as the ancestry of modern Western cemeteries lies in consecrated churchyards and church-controlled burial grounds. To many others, the cemetery has a degree of sacredness, but is less than that of the church. Yet others considered the cemetery has a sense of sacredness, in that it should be venerated, but for non-religious reasons. And all mourners in the study, including the non-visitors, considered the cemetery to be a very special place.

Many visitors value the various opportunities that a cemetery provides for continuation of their cultural traditions. To this end, cultural segregation of traditional funereal and commemorative activities is particularly important to many people of diverse backgrounds. Yet this choice has become less available in modern cemeteries developed within homogenizing concepts of non-denominationalism, or multiculturalism.

Evidently, for some mourners cemeteries are venues of important social support and assistance toward grief mitigation, through mutual sharing of personal bereavement experiences with other visitors. Close and highly valuable friendships are found to have developed in dedicated cemetery compartments among empathetic mourners of specific cultural and social groups, such as mothers and those of non-English speaking backgrounds and non-Christian faiths.

To mourners, general heritage values include cultural heritage, and local and family histories. The concept of heritage is recognized as being significant to different communities, groups, and individuals, depending on their specific human values and attitudes and the nature of the heritage resource [5]. Perceived heritage values of a cemetery tend to be recognized more by those with outside interests and little or no direct emotional, spiritual, or financial investment in the particular cemetery.

THE MEMORIAL

A cemetery memorial is here defined as any plaque, monument, and/or other associated object within a cemetery, dedicated to commemorating the life and/or marking the death of a decedent.

The concept of permanence of a memorial is quite important, and personal shrines and cenotaphs are particularly significant in the lives of some bereaved people.

The study revealed that common values of cemetery memorials to visitors include a focal point of remembrance, cultural and personal expression, symbolizing the decedent, identifying the location of remains, and recording family history. Mourners' own expressions of these values of memorials are presented in the following sections.

Focal Point of Remembrance

All visitors in the study referred either directly or indirectly to the respective memorial's value as a focal point for remembrance of the decedent, and all engaged in some form of commemorative activity at the location of the memorial.

> I think it's critical that we do remember where our deceased go and that they
> do have memorials and plaques to remember them by.
>> *25-year-old, Australian Catholic grandson,*
>> *bereaved 1 year*

Some individuals referred to feelings of distress on discovery that the bodies of people significant to them lay in unmarked graves. And in at least one case, this emotion was strong enough to spur remedial action.

> We found that one of our blokes was buried in a country cemetery in an
> unmarked grave. . . . We got a bronze plaque and a retired Anglican army

padre—a chaplain who was also a Vietnam Veteran—who'd actually buried him; and we had a memorial service there. Then we went into the local Returned Servicemen's League and had our few beers and what-have-you. It's a respect for the man.

62-year-old, Australian non-religious husband,
bereaved 4½ years

Some Christians (Catholic and Protestant) expressed disapproval of the scattering of cremated remains, due to this increasing practice averting a required focal point for remembrance.

[Our] next door neighbor . . . was cremated and his ashes were scattered over Botany Bay. We couldn't believe that. We knew it was his wish, but [his wife] wasn't happy with it afterwards. She felt that there was nowhere she could relate to him after his death, to even take a flower. She was really sorry she did that. So that's why I think the cemetery is very important.

40-year-old, Italian Catholic son,
bereaved 3 years

Cultural and Personal Expression

Several mourners referred either directly or indirectly to the memorial's value in facilitating cultural or personal expression. Choices in basic types or styles of memorials and individual personalization may reflect specific religious or other cultural traditions, or even preferences of the deceased.

Distinct styles of monuments are usually evident and may differentiate several specific cultural groups within most general cemeteries. Even within general monumental areas of mixed faiths and nationalities, specific differences in monumental styles and symbols are evident among differing ethnicities.

A Jewish sister revealed a family dilemma with the complexity of expressing both cultural and personal identity through a fitting memorial.

You know, when an elderly grandparent dies you have to pick a straight monument, maybe black or a gray marble. But in Jewish religion, you know that there's a Star of David and there are certain things that go on it; it goes to a form, I guess. It's the same with Greeks or Italians. But when you're talking about somebody like [my brother], who was a unique individual, you couldn't just give him a black piece of marble with the Star of David and normal writing; you have to go a little bit different, because that's the kind of person that he was.

37-year-old, Australian Jewish sister,
bereaved 8 months

Despite their general popularity in contemporary Western society, physical memorials are not considered significant within all cultures. Some forms of Buddhism, for example, do not advocate memorialization.

You can have a memorial if you want. There's no hard and fast rule; it's just an option, you know. But we don't focus on material things, you see. We might just plant a tree. For example, where my Dad was cremated, we just planted a flowering tree where the funeral pyre was lit. Now that tree blooms.

59-year-old, Sri Lankan Buddhist
daughter, bereaved 3 months

Many mourners consider it particularly important to fulfill the specific wishes of the deceased, and some consider fulfilling decedent's wishes to be more important than upholding traditional practices.

Locating the ashes in a particular place is not all that important any more. I used to think it would be, but not for [my partner]. If it were for my mother, then it would be a different story. But because [my partner] didn't worry about it, it doesn't worry me as much. I feel it's important to do what the person wanted done with their remains.

34-year-old, Australian Anglican
de facto wife, bereaved 3 years

Symbolizing the Decedent

Some visiting mourners referred either directly or indirectly to the memorial's value as a symbol of the decedent. To some visitors, it is most important that the memorial reflects aspects of the decedent's personality.

[My brother] was artistic, creative and young; and these were things that we wanted to reflect in the monument.

37-year-old, Australian Jewish sister,
bereaved 8 months

And to some, the memorial may also serve as a physical representation of the decedent, to which the expression of affection may be directed.

I give his headstone a kiss . . . I never, ever go away without giving [my grandson's] headstone a kiss.

60-year-old, Australian non-religious
grandmother, bereaved 5 years

Identifying the Location of Remains

Several visitors referred to the memorial's value in identifying the physical location of the remains of the decedent.

There's just a bronze plaque; the cremated remains are in the lawn and the bronze plaque is on the concrete plinth. . . . I mean, that's where the remains are, right in front of you. I have actually put my hand on the grass while I'm talking to her knowing that the remains are directly underneath there.

35-year-old, Australian non-religious
granddaughter, bereaved 4 years

I think putting a permanent marker there is important. Well, that's where her body is, and it was important to her. . . . So it's important I think; it's very important. When I die, I think I'd like somebody to say, "Look; he's buried there."

> *51-year-old, Australian non-religious husband,*
> *bereaved 2 months*

Recording Family History

Some mourners noted the respective memorial's value in recording their family's history.

His name is always going to be written down and not forgotten, somewhere for the grandchildren . . . to go and visit.

> *25-year-old, Australian Catholic grandson,*
> *bereaved 1 year*

Permanence

A few female visitors, of diverse beliefs, commented on the permanent status of memorials. Each considered a temporary marker to be essential, prior to installation of a permanent memorial.

The grave was not finished until the stone monument replaced the temporary wooden cross, some months later. As soon as that was done, we went together and I said, "He's at rest now; nobody else can hurt him."

> *60-year-old, Australian non-religious*
> *grandmother, bereaved 5 years*

But at least one mother, having previously focused her affections on the temporary marker representing her child, then had mixed feelings about its replacement.

We're now looking at putting a monument there, but I love her cross. A lot of people I know feel that it would be nice if we could just leave the crosses there, because there's something about babies and just having a simple cross that just seems right. But at the same time, I'm very happy with what we've chosen for a monument. So yeah, it is important to me to have a final monument to her—the cross does feel a little bit temporary.

> *27-year-old, Australian Catholic mother,*
> *bereaved 10 months*

No Importance

But not all participants in the study saw any particular value to be derived from a cemetery memorial. Some informants were not cemetery visitors at all, though one had no option to visit as the decedent had been cremated and the remains scattered overseas.

In Australia, some 7% of cremated remains are scattered by crematoria authorities [6]. Scattering may occur either at the family's specific request, or by default owing to family apathy toward cremated remains and memorialization. Some consider cremated remains to be sanitized matter which, unlike bodily remains, do not require final disposition or memorialization in a cemetery or elsewhere [7]. One informant put it this way:

> Before I'd gone through the death of [my partner], I always thought that placing cremated remains was very important. I didn't understand why some people wanted to scatter ashes. Now I understand how people can forget about them and even leave them at the crematorium. It is just a lot easier not to think about it.
>
> *34-year-old, Australian Anglican*
> *de facto wife, bereaved 3 years*

Personal Shrines

As well as regularly visiting and maintaining respective graves, some mourners also maintain home cenotaphs or personal shrines to their decedents.

A large dresser, which must be negotiated on entering or leaving the bedroom of an elderly Italian Catholic widow in the study, serves as a shrine to her late husband. Decorating the dresser are numerous items including photographs, a remembrance card and vigil lamp. Rather than any endeavors to reconstruct an alternate life following the death of her husband, she chooses to focus her thoughts on him every day and to retain his presence within their bedroom.

In the home of a middle-aged daughter of no specific faith, but whose mother was Catholic, the prominent dining-room sideboard serves as a shrine to her parents. One side features a large photograph of her late mother surrounded by several personal items, including spectacles, other photographs, and memorabilia. The other side features a large photograph and similar personal items relating to her late father, including a container with one half of his cremated remains—the other half being interred in the family grave with the body of her mother. Her thoughts are daily focused on her parents through the shrine, which her husband and children also eat in front of everyday.

Summary of Memorial Values

A permanent memorial proclaims the significance of the life of a decedent and may hold several short and long-term values to cemetery visitors. These values include providing a focal point for remembrance, facilitating cultural or personal expression, fulfilling the decedent's wishes, symbolizing the decedent, identifying the location of the remains, and recording family histories.

Perhaps the most significant value of a cemetery memorial is in providing a specific focal point for remembrance of the decedent. And where a memorial is held as symbolic of a decedent, maintenance of the memorial may represent continuing personal care for the decedent.

Clegg also found memorials to be important aids toward personal expression of loss.

> When a memorial marks the site of a deposition, then for months and sometimes for a few years, it provides a real focus for grief. It is the place where the mourner can re-experience and express the pain of the loss at a time when he or she chooses to visit it. . . . A static memorial in a suitable environment gives mourners the chance of going to a chosen site as and when they wish, and thus enables them to exercise some control over their expression of the loss [8, p. 3].

Memorials also facilitate cultural and personal expression through the choice of basic type, location, and individual style. And this choice may reflect family cultural traditions or the personality of the decedent. Ultimately, conglomerates of distinctly styled monuments tend to distinguish cemetery compartments utilized by specific cultural groups.

Despite their general popularity, physical memorials are not considered to be significant among all cultural groups, suggesting that specific social obligation is an important determinant of the significance of a memorial. Generally, among those opting for cremation, much less emphasis is placed on the interment site and memorialization than occurs among those who choose burial.

Leaving a grave unmarked, or scattering cremated remains, is certainly convenient to some mourners, particularly in the short-term. But research in Australia, Britain, and the United States suggests these actions can hinder grief resolution and evoke emotions of distress, particularly among those for whom identification of a point of focus and/or historical recording are particularly important [4, 8, 9]. Cable, for example, considers that:

> The reality is that most survivors need a place to focus their grief—a place for memorialization. . . . If a family talks of scattering the ashes, it is wise to raise questions as to where they would go in three years if they wanted to feel close to the deceased and deal with any remaining grief issues [9, p. 24].

And Clegg also suggests that faithfully implementing the expressed wishes of the deceased, in this respect, may not necessarily be in the best interests of the bereaved.

> Occasionally, individuals . . . say they don't want money spent on a funeral . . . the intention is to save the family needless expense. However, from another point of view, it totally denies the importance of the ritual and the psycho-logical dimension to death and grief, and if actually put into action, can deprive the family of the various processes which facilitate mourning and adjustment. Sometimes, I feel these decisions are made because there is no real knowledge of what loss is like, and although families derive comfort

from carrying out the stipulated wishes, later, they may come to regret the lack of a grave, gravestone or memorial plaque [8, p. 2].

A memorial, to identify the location of the remains and provide a focal point of remembrance, and that facilitates cultural and personal expression of the bereaved, is evidently of great importance to most mourners endeavoring to work through common grief issues.

VISITATION

While the identified reasons for visiting focus on why the bereaved visit cemeteries, individual values of visiting relate to what is personally gained from the experience. Common personal values of cemetery visitation relate to mitigating personal losses through fulfilling duties and obligations, maintaining emotional bonds, and seeking solace.

Just over half of the visitors in the study specifically reported some degree of euphoria or catharsis associated with visiting the cemetery.

> I look forward to it actually; I look forward to going to the cemetery.
> *66-year-old, Maltese Catholic husband,*
> *bereaved 4½ years*

> In the first year or two, you feel that it benefits yourself to go to the cemetery.
> *45-year-old, Australian non-religious female*
> *secret-lover, bereaved 3 years*

> I come down to the cemetery because it makes me feel really good. . . .
> Usually, I come here crying and leave feeling better.
> *27-year-old, Australian Catholic mother, bereaved 10 months*

And several mourners considered that significant value was to be gained from sharing personal experiences with other bereaved visitors.

> I organize other mothers to be there, so we can be together and have a chat. . . .
> If I'm on my own, I spend the time specifically with [my son], but if I'm with other mums, we just get together in the sun and we sit there and just talk and talk to our kids.
> *33-year-old, Australian Catholic mother,*
> *bereaved 2 years*

Some bereaved people recognize a benefit of occasional visits, but consider frequent visitation to be unnecessary. And yet others, who may visit infrequently, consider they derive no personal value from their visits.

> I think [my daughter] would feel like we do: that we wouldn't want the family coming up all the time. I'd rather they got on with their own lives. You can remember without going to the cemetery, of course.
> *64-year-old, Australian Uniting father,*
> *bereaved 3 years*

I just don't believe that's where she is. I don't see it as a rite of passage or anything like that, for me to be there. It doesn't help me get anywhere and it doesn't remind me of [my daughter]; I have enough ways to do that.

37-year-old, Australian Baptist father,
bereaved 3 years

Within the study, actual and potential negative values of visitation were also identified. While some infrequent visitors felt that visiting more frequently could be detrimental, some non-visitors considered that any visitation might have a negative emotional impact.

I don't think that I'm ever going to be a frequent visitor; it is far too traumatic. . . . When I'm there, I identify with him and his last moments of pain. It's not a future thing; it's definitely a past thing, and a definite loss for me.

37-year-old, Australian Jewish sister,
bereaved 8 months

The main personal values of visitation closely relate to major reasons for visiting. The majority of mourners visiting a cemetery reported the experience to be personally beneficial, in that, from visiting they derive a sense of well-being.

This chapter summarized common personal values of funerals, cemeteries, memorials, and grave or memorial visitation to mourners of various social and cultural backgrounds. Cemeteries were found to hold degrees of sacredness, cultural values, social support, heritage, and remembrance values to various mourners.

The concluding chapter will review contemporary notions of working through personal grief and the place of the cemetery within such a context.

REFERENCES

1. P. Bachelor, *Cemetery visitors in Australia,* Eleventh National Conference of the Australian Cemeteries & Crematoria Association, Alice Springs, August 30-September 3, 1998.
2. R. Nicol, *The ritual of death in colonial South Australia,* Cummins Society, Adelaide, 1992.
3. J. A. Walter, *The revival of death,* Routledge, London, 1994.
4. P. Bachelor, *Cemetery visitation: The place of the cemetery in the grief process,* unpublished Ph.D. thesis, Charles Sturt University, Wagga Wagga, 2001.
5. M. C. Hall and S. McArthur, *Heritage management in Australia and New Zealand: The human dimension,* Oxford University Press, Melbourne, 1996.
6. Australian Cemeteries & Crematoria Association, Cremation in Australia, *ACCA News,* pp. 9-11, Autumn 1998.
7. R. G. E. Smith, Death care activities and providers, *American Cemetery, 69*(10), pp. 74-79, 1997.

8. F. Clegg, *The psychological importance of memorials,* New Zealand Master Monumental Masons' Association, Cemetery Planning Seminar, Wanganui, August 7-8, 1991.
9. D. G. Cable, No place to visit and grieve: Potential problems in scattering ashes, *ACCA News*, pp. 23-24, Summer 1999.

CHAPTER 14
Working Through Grief

Part C has so far presented key findings of the qualitative Bereavement Study, including reasons for visitation and non-visitation, major visitation activities and emotions, changes to visitation patterns, and various values of the cemetery to mourners of socially and culturally diverse backgrounds. This concluding chapter now reconsiders the notion of grief-work, and specific values of the cemetery relating to this process.

Here, cemetery visitation emerges as a crucial aspect of working through grief for a majority of mourners within Western societies, and is found to be particularly important in the early stages of bereavement. We also conclude that this behavior is driven by a combination of complex social, cultural, and psychological factors.

GRIEF-WORK

It is well recognized that the term "grief-work," which was first proposed by Freud, remains an important concept in our understanding of bereavement within Western societies [1-4].

Worden promotes the idea of grieving as something we do, rather than merely something that happens to us. He suggests we should therefore view grieving as an active rather than a passive process. And toward a successful bereavement outcome he proposes a series of tasks that he considers mourners need to undertake. His tasks of grieving are: first, to accept the reality of the loss; second, to work through the pain of grief; third, to adjust to an environment in which the decedent is missing; and finally, to emotionally relocate the decedent and move on with life [1].

In most cases of bereavement, the funeral is an important event toward the first of Worden's tasks of mourning in that it helps facilitate acceptance of the reality of the loss. But beyond the funeral, visiting the grave or memorial

167

then becomes the most significant practical bereavement activity of most Western mourners.

The majority of cemetery visitors therefore constitute mourners working through Worden's subsequent tasks. That is, they are working through the pain of grief, adjusting to an environment in which the decedent is missing, and they are emotionally relocating the decedent and moving on with their lives.

Working through the pain of grief, including making required psychosocial adjustments and moving on with life, commonly correlates to initially frequent but then progressively diminishing cemetery visitation.

Avoidance behavior, including refusal to visit an otherwise-accessible grave or memorial of a significant decedent, suggests some failure in working through the pain of grief. While at the other end of the behavioral spectrum, chronic frequent visitation is also indicative of a failure to adjust psychosocially and to move on with life.

But sometimes, chronic frequent visitation can be a conscious choice, such as among elderly widows. Walter points out, being urged to "let go" may in effect compound the grief of those who earnestly desire to keep the decedent as a significant part of their daily life [5].

Toward making what Parkes considers necessary adjustments, he notes that grief-work includes an attempt to make sense of the loss, or to fit it into one's set of assumptions about the world, or to modify those assumptions if need be. And he considers attempts to make sense of what has happened would seem to be one way of restoring what is lost, by fitting its absence into some super-ordinate pattern. But, he adds, if these attempts are unsuccessful, then the preoccupation will increase and may indeed become obsessive [3].

Within the Bereavement Study, failure to make sense of the loss of a significant other was identified as a significant factor in much frequent cemetery visitation.

When grieving, our assumptive world may be modified to incorporate concepts of the decedent in a fitting afterlife, and to facilitate meaningful communication with the decedent. Our idea of such a suitable afterlife may include a pre-existing notion of heaven or some other spiritual realm.

But concepts of an afterlife are evidently adopted or modified, as suggested by Parkes, to suit the needs of the mourner [3]. For example, bereaved parents visiting a grave within a cemetery section dedicated to the burial of children may choose to envisage their own child within a metaphysical playground, accompanied by the deceased children of other parents who visit the same site. As a distressed grandmother commenting on a similar concept said: "That's how I comfort myself. I don't think about whether it's true or not."

To more fully understand common phenomena of death, we must be prepared to suspend our logic. Saying goodbye to a dead body or coffin does not appear logical, but is nevertheless crucial to most mourners. And talking to our deceased at a grave or shrine, and numerous other spiritual concepts may also be quite illogical, but these activities and associations become very meaningful and important to most mourners. It is their own personal values and meanings that we must seek to understand and respect if we are to be at all helpful to other mourners.

Just what ideas, faith concepts, and practices we choose to help us through our grief are usually quite illogical. Nevertheless, a lack of logic does not invalidate the value of any ritual. As John Lennon sang: "Whatever gets you thru the night, 'salright, 'salright" [6].

In concluding this discussion, it is appropriate to recognize grief as a common universal human reaction to the loss of someone significant to the mourner. Grief typically comprises three or more recognized phases, including an initial trauma response (involving shock and disbelief), an intervening grief response (involving cognitive awareness and acute mourning), and an ultimate psychosocial transition (involving resolution, accommodation, and reconstruction).

Achieving a satisfactory psychosocial transition is the ultimate desirable outcome of working through grief. And grief-work is the sum of a mourner's endeavors toward achieving such a satisfactory bereavement outcome.

THE PLACE OF THE CEMETERY WITHIN CONTEXTS OF GRIEF

Social and individual values of the cemetery are highly subjective. Even general community values attributed to the cemetery through legislation and management regulations cannot reflect those of all interested parties, and too often do not even reflect the values of a majority of legitimate stakeholders.

Among recently bereaved cemetery visitors, personal values of the cemetery vary by the emotional significance of the decedent, the ethnicity of the family, the sex of the visitor, the method of disposition of the remains, any afterlife concept held by the visitor, and their progression or accomplishment at working through grief.

The primary service provided by the cemetery and the rite through which the bereaved symbolically and physically enters is the funeral. This social acknowledgment of the humanity and mortality of the decedent can be an important catalyst of grieving their loss. The funeral often helps the bereaved in accepting the reality of a specific death, and commonly facilitates an essential transition from a mourner's initial trauma response to the loss.

The cemetery therefore becomes significant within the context of personal grief at this transition to the intervening grief response, which involves cognitive awareness and acute mourning. This significance persists to the mourner's ultimate psychosocial transition, involving resolution and accommodation of the loss, and reconstruction of one's life. Through these phases, the bereaved person typically works through the pain of grief, adjusts to an environment in which the decedent is missing, emotionally relocates the decedent, and eventually moves on with life.

Many mourners uphold the cemetery as a place of great emotional and spiritual significance, and a place to be respected for its sacredness, cultural significance, social support, heritage, and commemorative values. Visiting the cemetery becomes an important behavioral activity of many people holding these values. However, not all mourners are able to or chose to visit the cemetery. Some seemingly adopt personal concepts of grief-work that accommodate no cemetery visitation, while others endeavor to repress their grief.

Nevertheless, each year literally hundreds of millions of mourners around the world, find that the cemetery offers solace and a sense of personal well-being. The cemetery is a place that facilitates some degree of control over loss, allowing some escape from the anguish of separation. It is an important place where potentially stressful obligations may be expressed and resolved.

For most Western mourners, the cemetery becomes a crucial focal point for remembrance of their deceased, and it offers an antidote for unhealthy repression of grief. Major visitation reasons, activities and emotions all relate to continuing bonds with the deceased, and most cemetery visitors maintain a strong perception of visiting a decedent as a person.

As a crucial component of working through grief for many mourners, cemetery visitation evidently offers most value in the early stages of bereavement. Initially frequent visitation commonly allows the bereaved to work through and mitigate intense emotions, including grief and sadness, guilt, loss, loneliness, and anger. The perception of being in a decedent's presence can provide appreciable solace from the intense anxiety of separation, which is most commonly experienced in early bereavement.

Visiting the grave or memorial also allows emotions of grief to be mitigated through keeping a part of the decedent alive within the life of the mourner, and thereby facilitating a progressive emotional relocation. Conversely, deliberate avoidance of the cemetery denies mourners the potential therapeutic benefits of visitation.

The main societal value of Western cemeteries is evidently the personal commemoration of significant decedents. This value appears greater among females than males, and is more notable within some ethnicities, including Southern Europeans, than among Westerners such as Britons, North Americans, and Australians.

Cemetery visitation is clearly a high-participatory value-laden expressive activity, and a most significant observable behavioral activity of the recently bereaved. It is an important meaningful behavioral activity of literally hundreds of millions of mourners each year, and one driven by a combination of complex social, cultural, and psychological factors.

REFERENCES

1. J. W. Worden, *Grief counselling and grief therapy: A handbook for the mental health practitioner* (2nd ed.), Routledge, London, 1991.
2. T. Attig, *How we grieve: relearning the world,* Oxford University Press, New York, 1996.
3. C. M. Parkes, *Bereavement: Studies of grief in adult life* (3rd ed.), Penguin, London, 1996.
4. S. Freud, Mourning and melancholia, in *Sigmund Freud: Collected papers* (vol. 4) (J. Traviere, trans. 1959), Basic Books, New York, 1917.
5. J. A. Walter, *The revival of death,* Routledge, London, 1994.
6. J. Lennon, *Whatever gets you thru the night,* Lenono Music/BMG Music Publishing, 1974.

Glossary

A concise general glossary of terms associated with death, funerals, beliefs, cemeteries, and mourning

Adulation	Great praise, flattery or attention.
Anatomy	Science of dissection, or structure, of a body.
Ambivalence	Having co-existing opposites, e.g., love/hate relationship.
Ancestor	Person from whom one is descended.
Animism	Belief that all living and natural objects have souls.
Antecedent	Previous or preceding.
Anthropology	Study of humans, including physiology and/or culture.
Artifact	Item of human construction.
Ashes	Residue of fire; cremated remains.
Autopsy	Post-mortem examination or personal inspection.
Barrow	Ancient grave mound or tumulus.
Bereave	Lose someone or something of value.
Bereavement	State of loss (usually through death of someone significant).
Bereft	Deprived by bereavement.
Bier	Moveable frame on which coffin is placed during funeral.
Biopsychosocial	Interaction combining biological, psychological and social elements.
Bless	Declare or bestow divine favor.
Body	Physical structure of a person (or organism) whether dead or alive.
Buddha	Title given to Siddhattha Gotama, founder of Buddhism.
Buddhism	Philosophical religion partly derived from Hinduism around 5 B.C.
Burial	Process of placing a body in a grave or under the ground.
Cadaver	Dead body, or corpse.
Casket	Rectangular box in which corpse is buried (see Coffin).
Catacomb	Underground cemetery or system of crypts.
Catafalque	Fixed frame or device for supporting coffin while lying in state.
Catharsis	Release of emotional tension.
Catholic	Universal; of Roman Catholic Church.
Celebrant	One who performs a rite such as a funeral.
Cemetery	Burial ground, originally meaning "sleeping place."
Cenotaph	Monument or memorial where remains are interred elsewhere.
Cerecloth	Waxed cloth for wrapping a corpse.
Cerement	Any grave clothes.
Chapel	Building or place of worship, or where funeral services are conducted.

Charnel	Repository for corpses.
Charnel House	Building where corpses or bones are deposited.
Christ	Christian messiah; title given to Jesus of Nazareth.
Christian	Of or pertaining to Christ or his teachings.
Christianity	The Christian religion and its beliefs and practices.
Church	Body of all, or of specific Christians; building for worship meetings.
Clergy	Body of all persons ordained for Christian religious service.
Cleric	Member of the clergy.
Coffin	Narrow casket, contoured to minimize grave digging.
Columbarium	Niche wall for cremated remains; literally "pigeon-hole."
Commemorate	Honor a memory, or serve as a memorial.
Commit	To consign (as in the earth) or to put in custody (as in a niche).
Committal	Act of committing remains, etc.
Compartment	A cemetery section for specific use.
Condole	Share sympathy over a death or great loss.
Condolence	Expression of sympathy.
Consecrate	Dedicate to religious purpose, or declare sacred.
Conventional	Customary, or conforming to accepted rules.
Coronach	Gaelic lamentation or dirge.
Coroner	Officer who holds inquests into possible violent or accidental deaths.
Coronial	Of or relating to a coroner.
Corporeal	Of or for the body; physical; Somatic.
Corpse	Dead body.
Corpus	Body (usually dead).
Cortege	Funeral procession.
Creed	Summary of doctrine or philosophy.
Cremate	Decompose a corpse by fire.
Crematorium	Building for cremation, usually including furnace room and chapels.
Cremator	Furnace for reducing corpses to ash.
Crematory	(USA) Cremation facility; often a simple furnace without any chapel.
Crypt	Burial room, vault, or niche.
Cult	Religious worship system focused on a specific person or principle.
Culture	Distinctive system of beliefs and practices of a society.
Custom	Usual practice; traditional social convention.
Dead	Lacking life; Extinct.
Death	Ending of life in a body.
Decay	Decompose or breakdown to more stable elements.
Decease	Death.
Deceased	Dead; collective of those who have died.
Decedent	Deceased person.
Decompose	Decay or breakdown of a body into its constituent elements.
Deed	Document conveying a right (such as right of interment).
Descendent	A person descended from another.
Deity	Divine god or goddess; the creator.
Delusion	False belief that is clearly unrealistic.
Demographic	Statistical representation of a human community.
Denomination	Specifically identified (usually major) religious group.
Depression	(Psych.) Mood disorder characterized by persistent sadness and despair.
Die	Suffer loss of life; Perish.
Dirge	Lament for the dead.
Disembody	Separate or free from a body, such as the soul.

Disinter	Remove from earth or from a grave.
Dismal	Causing or displaying gloom or misery.
Dispose	Deal with, put in order, or be rid of.
Disposition	Arrangement or setting of order.
Divine	Of, from, like, or for a god.
Doctrine	Principle body of religious instruction and belief.
Dogma	Tenet or basic principle of belief or opinion.
Elegiac	Pertaining to an elegy or of elegies; lamentation or mournful.
Elegist	Author or orator of an elegy.
Elegy	Song or poem of lament.
Elysium	Field of rest or dwelling place of virtuous souls.
Embalm	Preserve a corpse from decay by any of various chemical processes.
Emotion	Potentially intense, internal feeling.
Empathy	Psychological identification with, or understanding of, a person or ideal.
Enshrine	Enclose in, or serve as, a shrine.
Entomb	Place in, or serve as, a tomb.
Epicedium	Funeral song.
Epitaph	Words written in memory of a deceased person, usually on grave.
Eternal	Without end; everlasting.
Ethnic	Of or belonging to a specific cultural group.
Ethnography	Descriptive account of a specific social or cultural group.
Ethnology	Study of comparative cultures of various people.
Eucharist	Christian sacraments commemorating last supper of Christ.
Eulogy	Oration or writing in praise, usually of deceased; Panegyric.
Euthanasia	Literally "good death"; the act of ending life to prevent suffering.
Exanimate	Having lost life or animation.
Exequies	Funeral rites; Obsequies.
Exhume	Dig out or remove from the ground.
Expire	Terminate; Die.
Extinct	Extinguished; no longer in existence; Dead.
Faith	Religious belief (or system of beliefs) without logical proof.
Fatal	Deadly, or resulting in death.
Fatality	Occurrence of death; a person killed.
Feng Shui	Chinese theory of harmony between humans, earth and heaven.
Fermentation	Biochemical decomposition, usually in absence of oxygen.
Floral	Of or pertaining to flowers.
Florist	Person who produces or supplies flowers.
Funeral	Process of burial or cremation and associated ceremonies.
Funeral Director	One who directs or undertakes funeral arrangements.
Funeral Home	Establishment where the dead are prepared for burial or cremation.
Funeral Parlor	Same as Funeral Home.
Funerary	Paraphernalia used at a funeral, or for funerals.
Funereal	Of or pertaining to a funeral or funerals.
Garden of Remembrance	Garden of memorials or in remembrance of specific lives or an event.
Gender	Constructed distinctions between masculinity and femininity (see Sex).
Genealogy	Line of decent from ancestor, or study of such.
Ghastly	Horrible or frightful.
Ghost	Spiritual being.
Gloom	Dark, melancholy or despondency.
Grave	Earthen hole for burial of deceased, may include monument.

Gravestone	Stone grave marker, usually inscribed; Tombstone or Headstone.
Graveyard	Burial ground or cemetery.
Grief	Emotional (including physical & psychological) response to bereavement.
Grieve	Cause or suffer grief.
Grim	Sinister, stern or ghastly.
Gruesome	Horrible or disgusting.
Hallow	Honor as holy; Consecrate.
Headstone	Stone set at head of grave.
Hearse	Vehicle for conveying coffin at funeral.
Heaven	Abode of God and angels; paradise; destiny of righteous souls.
Hell	Place of eternal damnation and torment of the unrighteous.
Hindu	Of or pertaining to Hinduism.
Hinduism	Complex religious/social system derived in India around 1,500 B.C.
Holy	Sacred; godly quality.
Homicide	Killing of a human by another.
Homily	Sermon or moralizing discourse.
Hospice	Organization devoted to offering palliative care to terminally ill patients.
Icon	Devotional image or statue representing a holy figure.
Imam	Islamic religious leader.
Immortal	Not mortal; living forever.
Incarnation	Take on, or embody, (human) flesh.
Incense	Sweet-smelling smoke used in religious ceremonies.
Inhume	Place into the earth; Inter.
Inquest	Coroner's inquiry into cause of death.
Inscription	Words carved into an object, or written on a monument.
Inter	Place into the earth; Inhume.
Interment	Act of placing into the earth.
Inurn	Place into an urn.
Inurnment	Act of placing in an urn.
Islam	Religion of Muslims, revealed through Mohamed prophet of Allah.
Jew	Person of Hebrew descent or whose religion is Judaism.
Judaism	Jewish religion, based on Mosaic and Rabbinical law.
Karma	Sum of good and bad actions determining fate in next incarnation.
Keen	Wailing for the dead; Irish lament.
Kerb	Surrounding or edge stones (of monument).
Lament	Expression of grief, especially a song or poem.
Lamentation	Act or process of lamenting.
Last rite	Catholic rite performed just prior to, or on the death of a person.
Ledger	(Monumental) Flat, horizontal gravestone.
Lethal	Pertaining to or causing death.
Lich-gate (Lych-)	Roofed entrance to burial ground.
Liturgy	Prescribed forms of religious ritual.
Malodorous	Foul smelling.
Mason	Person who cuts and erects stone; Stonemason.
Mass	Liturgical celebration of Eucharist in the Roman Catholic Church.
Mausoleum	Grand above-ground tomb.
Memorial	Commemorative plaque, monument, other object or custom.
Memorial Park	Modern park-type cemetery for interment and memorialization.
Memorialize	Commemorate, or dedicate in memory.
Miasma	Unwholesome vapor or atmosphere.
Milieu	Social setting or environment.

Monody	Ode of lament.
Monolith	Single stone monument.
Monument	Physical memorial; usually inscribed stone structure.
Morbid	Of death or gruesome matters, or showing such interest.
Morgue	Room or building for keeping corpses until burial or cremation.
Moribund	Point of death, or coming to an end.
Mortal	Subject to, or causing death.
Mortician	Funeral director, or undertaker.
Mortuary	Of or pertaining to death; Morgue.
Mosque	Islamic place of worship.
Mourn	Feel or express grief or sorrow.
Mourner	Person who mourns (for the deceased).
Mummify	Embalm a corpse and preserve as a mummy.
Mummy	Corpse preserved by embalming, especially ancient Egyptian.
Muslim	Follower of, or relating to, the Islamic religion.
Necrobiosis	Tissue decay in a body.
Necrolatry	Worship of the dead.
Necrology	Obituaries notice, or list of deceased.
Necromancy	Supposed communication with spirits of the dead.
Necrophilia	Morbid attraction, particularly erotic, to corpses.
Necrophobia	Abnormal fear of death or corpses.
Necropolis	Greek "City of Dead," or ancient cemetery.
Necropsy	Examination of a body after death; autopsy.
Neurosis	Mental disorder characterized by irrational or depressive activity.
Neurotic	Pertaining to, or suffering neurosis.
Niche	Shallow recess (such as in a wall) to hold ashes.
Noisome	Harmful, noxious or offensive.
Noxious	Harmful or unwholesome.
Obelisk	Tapering stone pillar monument, usually four-sided.
Obit	Date of death; obituary notice.
Obituary	Notice of death, or account of life of a decedent.
Obsequies	Funeral rites; Exequies.
Ordain	Appoint to Christian ministry, or confer holy orders on.
Orthodox	True or correct; pertaining to Eastern Orthodox Church.
Ossuary	Receptacle for bones of deceased.
Pagan	Derogatory term for non-Christian.
Pall	Cloth spread over coffin or tomb.
Pallbearer	Bearer or escort of coffin at funeral.
Palliate	Appear to mitigate or alleviate (such as pain or symptoms).
Palliative	Anything used to alleviate (especially of pain in terminally ill patients).
Panegyric	Written or oral statement of high praise; Eulogy.
Parish	Area presided over by a specific church and clergy.
Pastor	Minister or spiritual guide of a church or congregation; shepherd.
Pastoral	Pertaining to a pastor or congregation.
Pathogenic	Of or causing disease.
Pathology	Scientific study of disease.
Penance	Sacrament including confession, punishment and absolution for sin.
Perfunctory	Performed routinely without concern; superficial.
Perish	Suffer loss of life; Die.
Perpetual	Eternal; continuing forever.
Perpetuity	State or quality of being perpetual.

Personality	A person's unique set of consistent behavioral traits.
Phenomenon	Remarkable incident or object of perception.
Phobia	Irrational fear of specific objects or situations.
Physical	Of or concerning the body; Somatic.
Piety	Quality of being pious.
Pious	Religiously devout or virtuous.
Plaque	Memorial tablet, often metallic.
Posterity	Descendants or succeeding generations.
Posthumous	Occurring after a death.
Post-mortem	After death, as in examination of body.
Prayer	Request made or thanks given to a god or object of worship.
Preneed	Before need (as in pre-purchase of one's own grave or funeral).
Priest	Ordained Catholic, Orthodox or Anglican minister.
Procession	Body of people or vehicles moving in orderly succession.
Protestant	Non-Roman Catholic or Eastern Orthodox Christian, of Reformation.
Psychosis	Mental disorder including delusions and loss of reality.
Psychosocial	Interaction combining psychological and social elements.
Psycho-sociocultural	Interaction combining psychological, social and cultural elements.
Psychosomatic	Somatic illness caused or aggravated by mental stress.
Psychotic	Pertaining to or suffering psychosis.
PTSD	Post-Traumatic Stress Disorder; disturbed behavior attributed to trauma.
Purgatory	Place where deceased Catholics expiate their sins.
Putrefaction	Process of bodily decomposition.
Putrescent	In or of the process of decomposition.
Putrid	Decomposed or rotten.
Pyre	Pile of solid fuel for cremating a corpse.
Qualitative	Of or measurable by quality.
Quantitative	Of or measurable by quantity.
Rabbi	Jewish teacher or religious leader.
Reincarnation	Rebirth of the soul in another somatic form.
Relic	Object of value or interest from a past age.
Religion	Belief in deity; expression of faith or system of worship.
Religious	Of or pertaining to a religion.
Remains	What is left (of a body after death, burial or cremation).
Remembrance	Act, process or object of or for remembering.
Repose	At rest, sleep or peace.
Requiem	Mass or music for the repose of the dead.
Requiescat	Wish or prayer that deceased may rest in peace.
Respects	Deferential esteem; regard or honor shown to another.
Resurrect	Rise from the dead; return to life.
Rite	Religious or customary observance or act.
Reverend	Title of a cleric.
Sacrament	Religious ceremony or solemn rite.
Sacred	Exclusively dedicated to religious use, or made holy.
Sacrilege	Violation or misuse of something sacred.
Sanctify	Set apart or observe as holy; consecrate.
Sarcophagus	Stone coffin, or casket-shaped monument.
Sect	Religious division or minor denomination.
Sectarian	Of or pertaining to a sect.
Secular	Not spiritual or bound by religion.

Sentiment	Thought, opinion or mental feeling.
Sentimental	Of sentiment; showing emotion rather than reason.
Sepulchral	Of or pertaining to a sepulcher.
Sepulcher	Rock or stone grave or vault.
Sepulture	Act of burying or interment.
Sermon	Religious or moral discourse.
Service	Intangible product provided to meet need; ceremony of worship.
Sex	Biologically-based attributes of male and female (see Gender).
Sexton	Churchyard caretaker and gravedigger.
Shrine	Sacred chapel, altar or grave for commemoration.
Shroud	Cloth (usually white) in which corpse is wrapped for burial.
Socialization	Acquisition of norms and behaviors expected within a specific society.
Society	Communal group or persons sharing common interests or attributes.
Sociocultural	Interaction combining social and cultural elements.
Solace	Comfort or relief from distress.
Somatic	Of the body; corporeal; physical.
Somber	Dismal; solemn; gloomy.
Sorrow	Emotional distress in response to loss.
Soul	Part of one's conscious being, thought to be independent of the body.
Spirit	Supernatural, incorporeal being; Soul.
Spiritual	Of or pertaining to the spirit as opposed to matter.
Spirituality	Non-traditional, experiential-based form of religion, often eclectic.
Stress	Response to any perceived threat to one's homeostasis or well-being.
Stagnant	Motionless; showing no activity.
Suicide	Intentional killing of oneself.
Stonemason	Person who cuts and erects stone, including monuments.
Survivor	One who continues to live.
Symbol	Object conventionally regarded as representing something else.
Sympathy	Feeling of sorrow with another.
Synagogue	Jewish place of worship or assembly.
Theism	Belief in the existence of a God or gods.
Theory	System of interrelated concepts used to explain a set of observations.
Tradition	Custom or belief passed down by a community.
Transcendent	Surpassing human experience.
Tribute	Thing said, done or given as mark of respect or affection.
Thanatologist	Person who studies or applies thanatology.
Thanatology	Study of death and its associated practices and phenomena.
Tomb	Grave or vault dug in ground or cut from stone.
Tombstone	Stone tomb marker, usually inscribed; Gravestone.
Tradition	Established custom; handed-down belief or practice.
Tribute	Words, action or object given as a mark of respect.
Tumulus	Ancient burial mound or barrow.
Undertaker	One who undertakes funeral arrangements; Mortician or Funeral Director.
Urn	A vase-like receptacle (for cremated remains).
Vault	Underground chamber; stone, concrete or brick grave.
Vigil	Nocturnal devotion; staying awake to watch or pray.
Wake	Watching over the dead; lamenting and ritual celebration.
Worship	Homage or reverence paid to a deity.
Wreath	Ring of flowers or floral materials.

Index

About the Author

Dr. Philip Bachelor is a recognized leader within the Australian cemeteries industry. His background includes landscape and resource management, business administration, and sociological bereavement research. He has been involved in the operation of cemeteries for some 23 years, including the past 15 years at Melbourne's Fawkner Crematorium & Memorial Park, leading the team responsible for developing and maintaining one of the world's largest cemeteries, providing around 100 burials and cremations and meeting the diverse cultural needs of some 40,000 bereaved visitors each week. Philip has reviewed cemetery operations in several countries, and is a regular writer and presenter on visitation and an advocate of understanding and accommodating mourners' needs. He is honorary Secretary and past President of the Cemeteries & Crematoria Association of Victoria, and honorary Secretary of the Centre for Grief Education in Melbourne. He is a Fellow of the Australian Institute of Horticulture, the Environment Institute of Australia and New Zealand, and the Australian Institute of Management; and a member of the Royal Society of Victoria.